Cloth Dolls

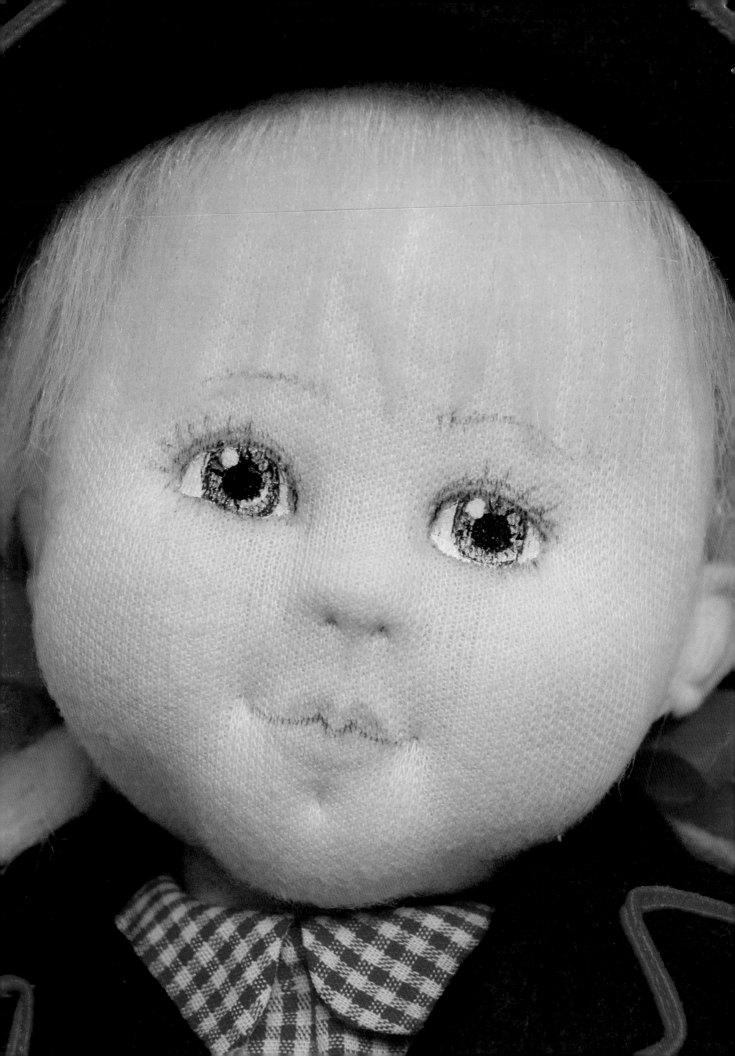

BRENDA BRIGHTMORE

Cloth Dolls

kp **kp books**
An imprint of F+W Publications, Inc.

©2004 Brenda Brightmore

First published in North America in 2005 by KP Books

kp books
An imprint of F+W Publications, Inc.

Our toll-free number to place an order or obtain
a free catalog is (800) 258-0929.

Library of Congress Catalog Number: 2004105217

ISBN: 0-87349-871-2

Designed and edited by David Porteous Editions

Printed in Singapore by Star Standard

Contents

Preface

I have been making cloth dolls for longer than I care to remember. I first started making dolls as a hobby when I was a child, then later for my two daughters and now for my granddaughter, Amy.

From the beginning, the dolls were all my own work and ideas, constructed using the tried and tested method of try and try again until it looked right. If ever I used magazine or commercial patterns I felt compelled to paint my own faces on the finished dolls to personalise them.

The dolls I make vary from cute babies to demure little girls and cheeky young boys. I am totally self-taught, and I use a variety of materials in the construction of the dolls and their clothes. I often spend a lot of my time planning, researching and sourcing the different fabrics I use.

My favourite part of doll making is forming the heads and painting the faces. It is at this point that you begin to see the doll's individual character and personality shining through.

The dolls I create range in size from tiny 5cm (2in) up to a 56cm (22in) Flapper doll, Poppy.

In 1995 I was accepted as a member of the British Doll Artists Association, and since that time my dolls have found a worldwide audience.

Brenda Brightmore

Making the Dolls

Before you make any of the dolls in this book, please read the following notes carefully.

Patterns and templates

None of the patterns or templates in this book has to be enlarged or reduced, and most of them can be traced straight from the page. Sometimes only half the pattern of some of the larger pieces is shown, but these pieces are clearly marked 'place on the fold', indicating that the straight edge of the pattern should be placed against the folded edge of the fabric. In addition, simple oblongs – used for skirts and cuffs, for example – are not shown full size, but the measurements are given.

Make accurate card copies of all the pattern pieces. Always make them full size, even when only half the pattern is shown, because it will make placing and cutting out easier.

Transfer all marks and instructions onto the card templates, and punch small holes where indicated for the placement of joint holes, openings and darts. Remember to write the name of the doll on the pieces of card so that you can identify them easily.

Most pieces have a seam allowance of 5mm (⅜in), which, conveniently, is the width of the presser foot on many types of sewing machine. A few of the pattern pieces are marked 'template', and these have no seam allowance. These are usually items – such as hands or small collars – for which it is easier to draw around the card template and then machine directly on the line and cut out after sewing.

Fabrics

No actual measurements for the amounts of fabric required are given. Fabric widths vary considerably, and many people will make more than one doll anyway. Only a very large doll will require more than 1 metre (1 yard) of fabric. At least two of the calico (muslin) dolls in this book can be cut from 70cm (27in) of fabric, and with careful cutting 50cm (20in) of Windsor Ponte or Comfort will make two needlesculpture baby dolls.

If you are buying some expensive fabric for a special project, lay out the card templates, taking into account the pieces that will have to be duplicated, and work out exactly how much you will need.

The calico (muslin) dolls are made from plain, un-bleached fabric, which is available in a range of qualities from most fabric shops. I usually wash and iron the material first to soften it and remove some of the seeds. Calico looks attractive in its natural state, but it is easy to tint or dye it if you prefer. The tiniest amount of tangerine powder dye – no more than one-eighth of a teaspoon – is enough to dye 1 metre (1 yard) a delicate flesh pink. Tans and browns need a more concentrated solution, so experiment with leftover bits.

Covered needlesculpture dolls need a stretchy 'skin' covering. Cotton stockinette is perfect: it clings to the shape of the base with no wrinkles, takes clear-drying tacky glue well, and its smooth surface is wonderful to paint on.

Stretchy Lycra fabrics are available, too, but because Lycra is a manmade fabric it does not cling like stockinette and may need more stitches to hold it in place. T-shirt cotton can also be used with care.

Needlesculpture dolls require a knit fabric with some stretch across the width. Most importantly, it must not run when stretched. The two fabrics I now use, Windsor Ponte and Windsor Comfort, are perfect for my patterns. You can, of course, use other fabrics if you wish. I made my first few needlesculpture dolls many years ago from a brushed nylon sheet I had bought from a jumble sale. Dressing-gown velour and T-shirt cotton also work well. Cotton stockinette is, however, far too stretchy for needlesculpture.

The type of fabric used for the clothes is given on each pattern. In general, use thin fabrics with small patterns. American cotton prints of the type sold for patchwork and quilting are lovely for doll clothes and can be purchased in small quantities.

Always buy the best quality felt you can find. If it is very thin, back it with iron-on interfacing first.

Fur fabric, which is used for many of the wigs, is available in different lengths and textures. The relevant pattern pieces are marked with arrows showing the direction of the pile. Draw around the patterns on the back of the fur fabric, and then use small, sharp scissors to cut out only the backing, never the pile.

Wigs made from mohair roving or purchased curly hair are not suitable for play dolls, which get a lot of wear and tear, but they can be used for dolls that older children keep for display or for adult collectors' dolls.

Cutting out

If a pattern piece has 'lengthwise of fabric' arrows on it, make sure the arrows are parallel with the selvage. If a pattern piece has 'maximum stretch' arrows, test the fabric first, then lay the pattern accordingly. This is essential when you are using stockinette and all needle-sculpture fabrics. Remember, too, that felt stretches more in one direction than the other, so lay all the pattern pieces in the same direction. Also, when you are cutting a fabric with a nap or one-way design, pattern pieces must all be laid the same way.

When a pattern piece is marked 'cut 2' or 'cut a pair' trace around the template and cut from a double layer of fabric laid with the right sides facing. When a pattern piece is marked 'cut 1' trace around it and cut from a single layer of fabric. When a piece needs to be cut twice – as with legs and arms – it will be marked 'cut 4' or 'cut 2 pairs'. Trace the first piece and then flip over the pattern and trace the second one in reverse to avoid mistakes on patterns where darts or joint holes are required on one side of a piece.

Pin all the traced shapes before cutting out to avoid slipping. Cut out right on the traced line – small pieces can 'grow' considerably if you are not careful. Mark all darts, dots and openings on the wrong side of the cut pieces and all top-stitching lines and face guides on the right sides.

Air-vanishing or water-erasable markers are available for doll-making. I always use a sharp ordinary lead pencil for tracing around patterns and for marking face guides. Draw lightly for face guides so that you can erase any inaccuracies.

Transferring face guides to fabric

Trace the pattern of the 'head front' or 'head centre' with the face guide onto a sheet of paper. Lay the cut fabric piece over the paper pattern with both right sides up. Pin the fabric to the paper. Use adhesive tape or Blu-Tack to attach the paper to a window, so that the light from behind will enable you to trace the face easily. Trace only the main guidelines – you can add eyelashes and other details later.

Sewing

Most of the sewing can be done by machine using a small stitch. I have rarely found it necessary to sew around a part twice – burst seams are usually the result of careless stuffing rather than weak sewing. You might, however, want to double-sew over stress points on the needlesculpture dolls.

Stay-stitching means working a row of machine stitching on a single layer of fabric, and it is used to prevent the fabric from fraying or stretching or sometimes to mark a seam allowance.

Ladder-stitch is used for invisibly closing openings in seams and to attach heads and limbs.

When you are making the clothes neaten the seam allowances and any other raw edges by oversewing

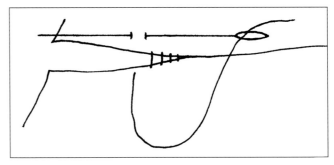

Use ladder-stitch for invisibly closing openings in seams and for attaching heads and limbs.

with a machine zigzag stitch (or use a serger). When you finish necklines with a bias strip sew the strip to the neckline with R.S. facing, using a narrow seam allowance. Press the strip to the inside of the neckline, turn in a narrow hem and stitch in place to cover the seam. In some cases hems can be made with fusible webbing instead of sewing. If you do not want to attempt tiny buttonholes use snap fasteners with decorative buttons on the outside.

Filling

Always use a good quality white toy filling. You will find several types and qualities available. The most expensive is a soft, silky filling, which is not necessarily the best one for dolls. I prefer a slightly coarser material, which stays in place better.

Special equipment

In addition to a basic sewing kit – small and large scissors, pins and needles and threads in appropriate colours – you will also need some special equipment.

Stuffing tools are a matter of personal preference, and you will probably need several. My favourites for many years were a long, thin screwdriver with a notch filed in the centre of the end of the blade, a wooden chopstick with a similar notch and a barbecue skewer. Now I use two of Barbara Willis's marvellous stuffing forks.

To make the needlesculpture dolls you will need ballpoint machine needles and extra long doll-making needles. You will also find cotton darners useful.

Use strong thread to attach limbs and to close openings. In addition, you will need white tacky glue and fray-check. You will need a hot-glue gun for some of the dolls.

Abbreviations	
R.S.	right side of fabric
W.S.	wrong side of fabric

Painting Faces

Materials and equipment

- 2 paintbrushes suitable for acrylic paints, a size 0 or 1 and a very fine one, size 00 or 000
- 2 permanent marker pens, black and brown with very fine tips, size 01
- Acrylic fabric paints, white, black and blue (or any other eye colour)
- Colour crayon pencils, clear red for lips and brown for shading
- Cosmetic blusher

Method

Do not dilute the paint or it may bleed into the fabric. Never allow acrylic paint to dry on your brushes or they will be ruined.

As a rule, the younger the child, the lower the eyes are placed on the face. The most common mistake is to place the eyes too high, but remember that a great deal of the upper head will be covered when the doll has hair. Another common mistake is to make the eyes too big, so when you are cutting out eye templates cut inside the drawn line or the eyes will 'grow' a little every time you trace around them.

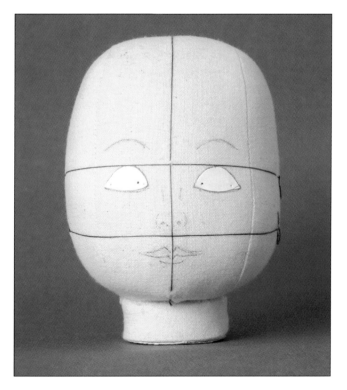

1 Using contrasting coloured thread, divide the face into four. Take the vertical thread from the crown to under the chin. Look straight at the face from the front and place the horizontal thread halfway down.

2 Practise drawing eye shapes on a scrap of thin card, cut them out and try them on the doll's face until you find the shape and size you think are most appropriate.

3 Fold a piece of scrap paper in half, trace your chosen eye shape on one side and cut it out through both thicknesses. You now have a pair of paper eyes, which can be moved about on the doll's face until you are satisfied with the position. Don't forget to mark the right sides to avoid confusion.

4 For a child doll the eyes are placed just below the horizontal line, about an eye's width apart. Draw around them lightly with a sharp pencil.

5 Divide the bottom half of the face with a second horizontal thread. The nose is drawn above this line, and the centre mouth line is about halfway between this line and the chin.

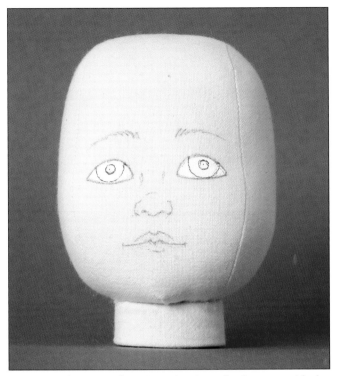

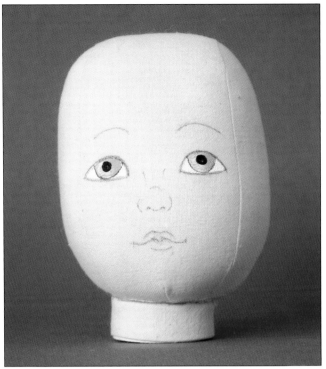

1 Remove the guide threads and redraw the features with the brown marker.

2 Paint the whole of the eye area white. It may need two coats. When the paint is completely dry, draw in the iris, using a small washer or button as a template. The iris should always touch the top or bottom eye lines – try to imagine a circle tucked under the eyelid.

3 Draw the pupil.

1 Paint the iris in your chosen colour, and while the paint is still wet blend in a little white paint at one side of each iris. Allow to dry.

2 Paint the pupils black. Leave to dry.

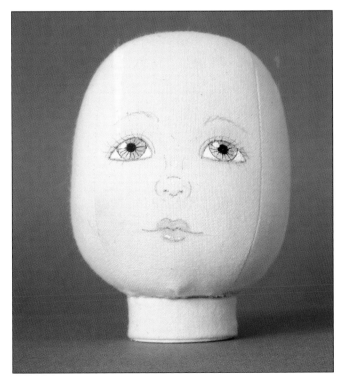

1 Use the black marker to draw fine radiating lines around the pupil.

2 Draw the eyelid crease with the brown marker.

3 Draw a few fine eyelashes with the brown marker.

4 Colour the mouth with the red crayon pencil. Colour the cheeks very gently with cosmetic blusher, applying it on a small piece of stuffing.

5 Dip the head of a straight pin in white paint and dot a white highlight beside each pupil, either both left or both right. Stroke a little white paint on the tip of the nose and on the bottom lip.

6 Shade under the eyebrows and the sides of the nose very lightly with the brown crayon pencil.

Calico Dolls

Amy and Andrew

The calico girl doll, Amy, stands 39cm (15½in) high and has the same endearing features as her cousin Andrew but easy-to-style hair. Her cotton summer dress, bar-strap shoes and large hair ribbon give her a quaint 1950s look.

Andrew, the 39cm (15½in) calico boy doll, has a bright-eyed, sweet painted face and a smart little outfit, but his fur fabric hair will not stay in place, no matter how often his mother brushes it.

Materials and equipment

- Unbleached or tinted calico

- Set of 3cm (1¼in) plastic joints (one set for each doll)

- Fur fabric for the wigs: long (for Amy) and shorter or rougher, animal-type (for Andrew)

- White polyester toy filling

- Stuffing sticks

- Fray-check

- Fabric paints, permanent markers, colour pencils (see page 10)

- Thin card to make templates of pattern pieces

- Basic sewing kit, including strong thread and threads to match all fabrics (including those for the clothes)

- Hair ribbon

Clothes

Pants Thin stockinette or T-shirt fabric; narrow elastic; narrow lace trim (for Amy's pants)

Underslip Cotton or polycotton fabric; broderie anglaise trim, 15mm (½in) wide; small button

Dress Cotton or polycotton print fabric; plain contrast fabric for collar and cuffs; snap fasteners; decorative buttons

Trousers Felt or thin wool cloth; strong snap fastener

Shirt Cotton or polycotton small check fabric; snap fasteners; decorative buttons

Necktie Plain cotton; narrow elastic

Socks Pair of child's socks, white (for Amy), grey or fawn (for Andrew)

Shoes Felt, with contrasting colour for the soles; strong cardboard; snap fasteners; decorative buttons (for Amy's shoes); embroidery thread (for Andrew's shoes)

Read *Making the Dolls* on pages 8–11 before you begin.

Styling Amy and Andrew's hair

Re-read the guidelines on page 8 before you cut fur fabric. Note the different cutting lines for Amy and Andrew. Face edge and nape are marked on the pattern pieces. Sew the darts at the crown of each piece. With R.S. facing, sew the wig front to the wig back. Turn R.S. out. Brush well to release any fur trapped in the seam. Place the wig on the doll and when you are satisfied with the position, sew it in place. Trim with small, sharp scissors.

1 Make a side parting, brush the hair to the side and hold with a stitch.

2 Trim level all round.

3 Sew ribbon to wig.

1 Brush all the hair upwards and trim the ends. Trim and brush until the desired length is achieved.

2 The back will require extra trimming. Fur wigs may be set with hair-spray.

1 Sew centre-front seam of body front.

2 Open out and finger press the seam. Stay-stitch the neck edge. Lay body front aside.

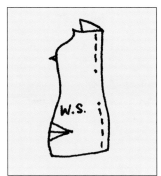

3 Sew centre-back seam of body back, leaving open between dots. Sew the hip darts.

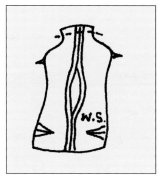

4 Open out and finger press the seam. Stay-stitch the neck edge. Lay body back aside.

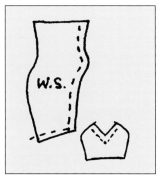

5 Sew centre-front seams of legs and open out. Stay-stitch ankle edges of legs and feet.

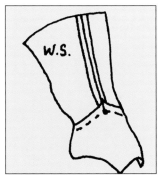

6 Sew feet to legs at ankle edges. Clip the seam allowance to centre dot.

7 With R.S. facing, sew centre-back seam of leg and foot.

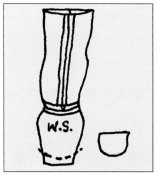

8 Flatten out foot with seam underneath and sew the toe in a curved line, using the toe guide.

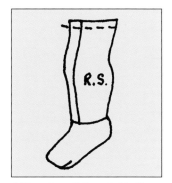

9 Turn legs R.S. out. Stuff firmly to within 2cm (¾in) of the tops. Align centre-back and centre-front seams and tack tops closed.

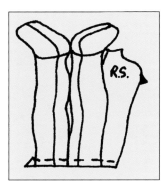

10 With R.S. facing, sew legs to lower edge of body front, leaving seam allowances free at both sides.

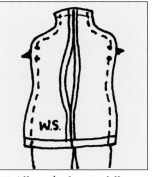

11 Allow the legs to fall forward. With R.S. facing, sew body back to body front, leaving open between dots for arm joints.

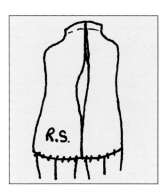

12 Turn body R.S. out. Slipstitch lower edge of body closed. Do not stuff body yet.

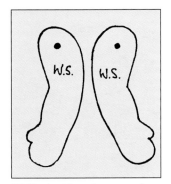

13 On insides of arms only, punch or clip small holes for joint pegs. Apply fray-check and allow to dry.

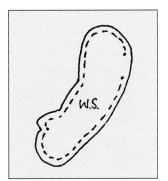

14 With R.S. facing, sew the arms together in pairs, leaving open between the dots. Turn the arms R.S. out.

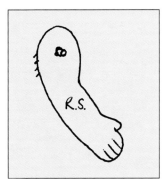

15 Stuff the hands softly and top-stitch the fingers. Insert the joints and stuff the arms. Ladder-stitch the openings.

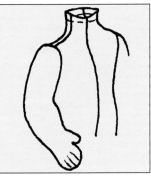

16 Joint the arms to the body. Tack the seam allowance of the neck to the inside. Stuff the body firmly and close the opening.

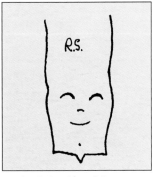

17 On R.S. of head front, trace the features lightly in pencil. Sew the chin dart.

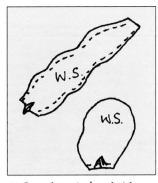

18 Sew darts in head sides. Stay-stitch both sides of head centre between dots and all neck edges.

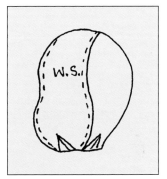

19 With R.S. facing, tack, then sew head sides to head centre. Clip seam allowance to stay-stitching at intervals to make fitting easier. Turn head R.S. out.

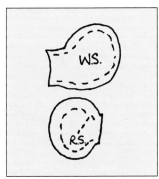

20 Sew around ears, trim seam closely and turn R.S. out. Stuff lightly, turn in seam allowance and top-stitch.

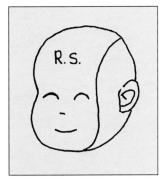

21 Stuff the head firmly and evenly, shaping with your hands as you work, and work a few cross threads across the neck opening. Slipstitch the ears in place.

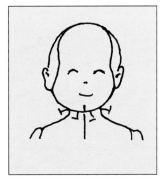

22 Pin, then ladder-stitch the head in place. Check the position of the features, erase and redraw them if necessary. See face painting (pages 10–11) to finish the face.

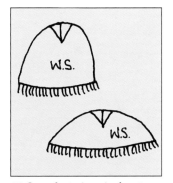

23 Sew darts in wig front and wig back. With R.S. facing, sew wig front to wig back, matching darts. Turn wig R.S. out.

24 Brush well to release any hair trapped in the seam. Follow the individual instructions for styling the wigs.

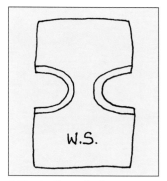

1 Pants. Turn the hem allowances on the leg openings to the inside and hem with a zigzag stitch. Plain hem for Andrew; trim with narrow lace for Amy.

2 Stitch one side seam. Make a casing along the waist edge, thread with elastic to fit the doll and sew the elastic into the remaining seam.

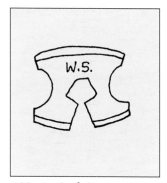

3 Underslip. With R.S. facing, sew backs to front. Neaten both back edges.

4 Neaten both lower edges of the facing.

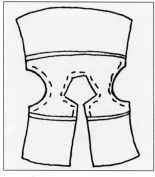

5 With R.S. facing, sew facing to slip at neck edge and armholes. Clip corners and curves. Turn R.S. out by gently easing the backs through the facings at the shoulders.

6 Stitch the side seams. Sew trim to the hem. Sew centre-back seam to dot. Turn R.S. out. Make a button and loop fastening at back neck.

7 Dress. With R.S. facing, sew front bodice to backs, open out and press seams.

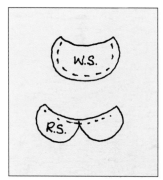

8 Sew the collars together in pairs, clip curves, turn R.S. out and press. Tack collars together at centre front.

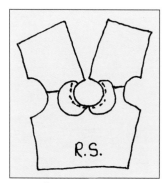

9 Matching centre fronts, sew collars to dress.

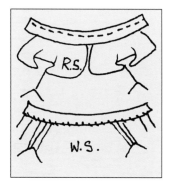

10 Sew the bias strip over the raw edges. Slipstitch neatly on the inside of the neckline. Press the back facings to the inside.

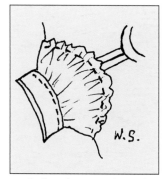

11 Gather the straight edges of the sleeves to fit the cuffs. With R.S. facing, sew cuffs to sleeves.

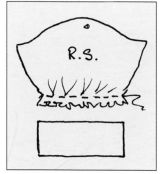

12 Gather the top edges of the sleeves to fit the armholes. With R.S. facing, sew the sleeves in place.

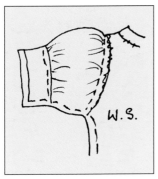

13 Sew the side seams of the bodice and sleeves. Finish the cuffs.

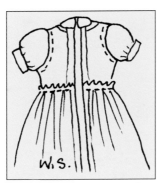

14 Gather the skirt to fit the waist of the dress. Sew the skirt in place.

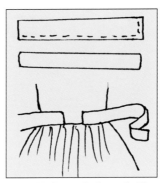

15 Fold the tie belts in half lengthwise, stitch, turn and press. Sew belts to bodice front.

16 Turn up and sew a 2cm (¾in) hem on the dress. Sew snap fasteners and decorative buttons to back opening.

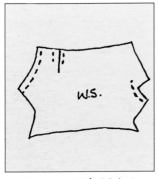

17 Trousers. With RS facing, sew the centre-back seam and centre-front seam to dot.

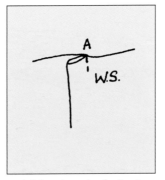

18 Make pleats in the back waist. Tack in place.

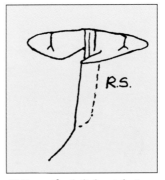

19 Press the left-front facing to the inside and top-stitch.

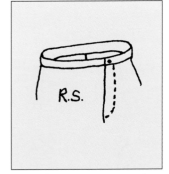

20 With R.S. facing, sew the waistband in place, press to the inside and slipstitch in place. Sew a snap fastener to the waistband.

21 Sew the crotch seam. Hem the trousers. Turn R.S. out.

22 Shirt. With R.S. facing, sew the back to the fronts. Neaten front edges.

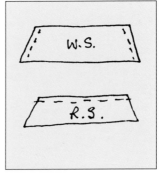

23 Sew both short edges of collar. Turn R.S. out, press and tack the open edge closed.

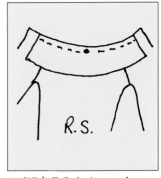

24 With R.S. facing and centre backs matching, sew collar to shirt. Using the bias strip, finish the collar as for dress.

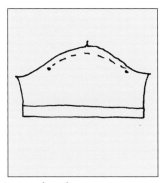

25 Gather the top edges of sleeves between dots. Press hem allowance of sleeves to W.S.

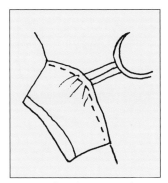

26 Sew the sleeves in place.

27 Sew the side seams of shirt and sleeves.

28 Hem the shirt and sleeves. Turn R.S. out. Sew snap fasteners and decorative buttons in place.

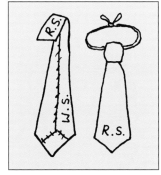

29 Necktie. Press all the seam allowances to the W.S. and hemstitch neatly in place. Turn 2cm (¾in) over at the top and stitch down to form a loop for the elastic. Make a false knot and stitch in place.

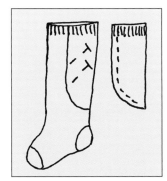

30 Socks. Cut two socks from the child's socks, using the top as the open edge. Sew the back seam with a stretch stitch. Turn R.S. out.

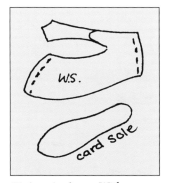

31 Amy's shoes. With one shoe inner and one shoe outer facing, sew centre-front and centre-back seams.

32 Turn shoe R.S. out. Gather all round close to lower edge. Insert cardboard sole and pull up gathers just enough to hold in place. Work a few stitches over the sole.

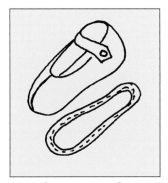

33 Gather all round the felt sole cover close to the edge, place the second cardboard sole inside and pull up gathers tightly. Ladder-stitch the covered sole in place.

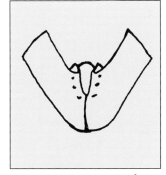

34 Andrew's shoes. With R.S. facing, sew centre-front seam to dot. Open out and press facings to the inside. Sew the tongue in place.

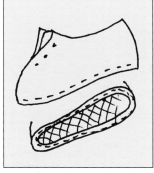

35 With R.S. facing, sew centre-back seam. Turn R.S. out. Finish shoe sole as for Amy's shoe.

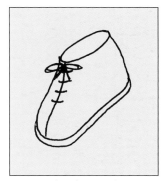

36 Lace the shoe with embroidery thread.

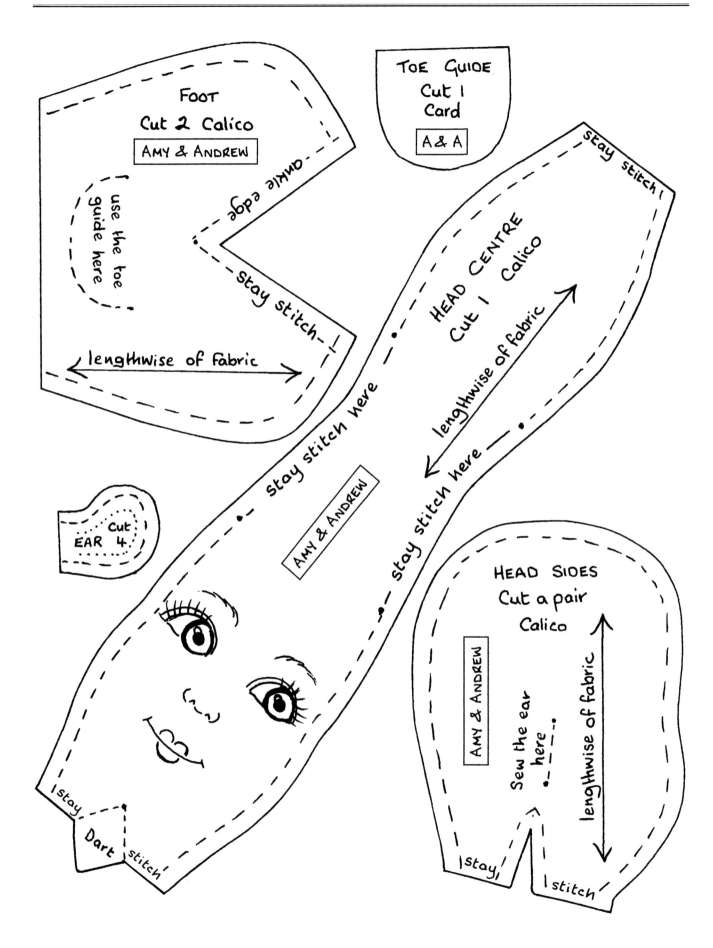

FOOT
Cut 2 Calico
AMY & ANDREW

use the toe guide here

ankle edge

stay stitch

lengthwise of fabric

TOE GUIDE
Cut 1
Card
A & A

HEAD CENTRE
Cut 1 Calico

stay stitch

lengthwise of fabric

stay stitch here

stay stitch here

AMY & ANDREW

Cut EAR 4

stay

Dart

stitch

HEAD SIDES
Cut a pair
Calico

AMY & ANDREW

Sew the ear here

lengthwise of fabric

stay

stitch

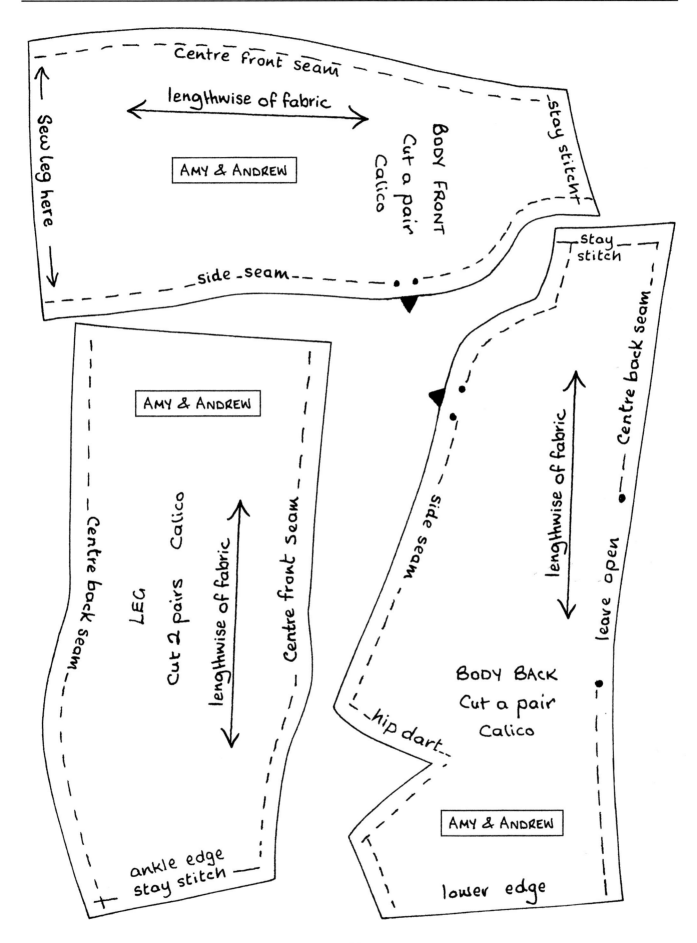

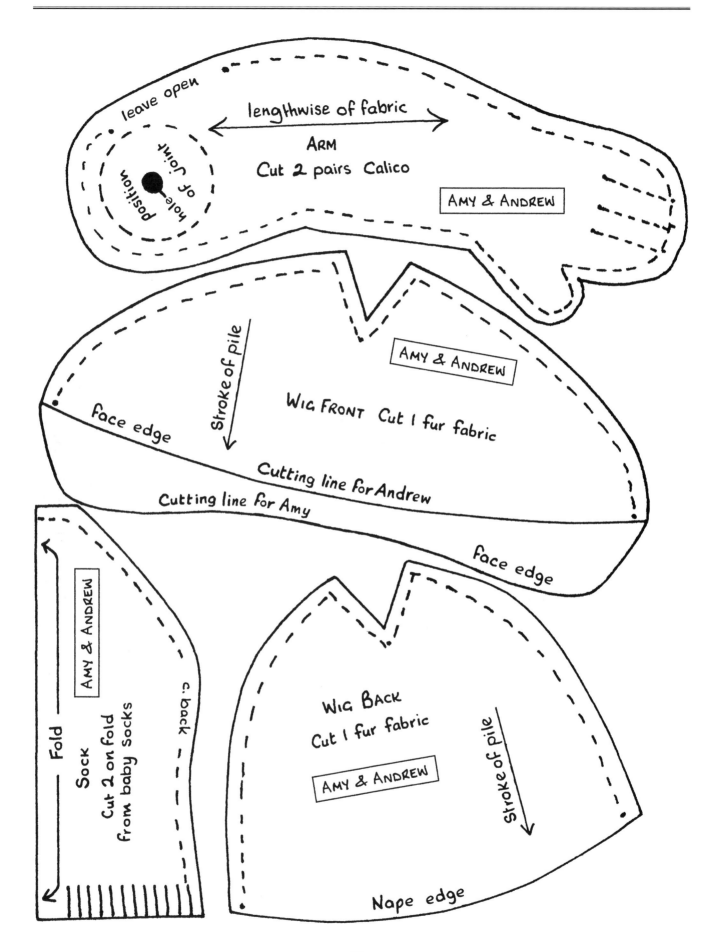

leave open

lengthwise of fabric

ARM
Cut **2** pairs Calico

position of joint
hole of joint

AMY & ANDREW

Stroke of pile

face edge

WIG FRONT   Cut 1 fur fabric

AMY & ANDREW

Cutting line for Andrew

Cutting line for Amy

face edge

Fold

Sock

AMY & ANDREW

Cut 2 on fold
from baby socks

c. back

WIG BACK
Cut 1 fur fabric

AMY & ANDREW

Stroke of pile

Nape edge

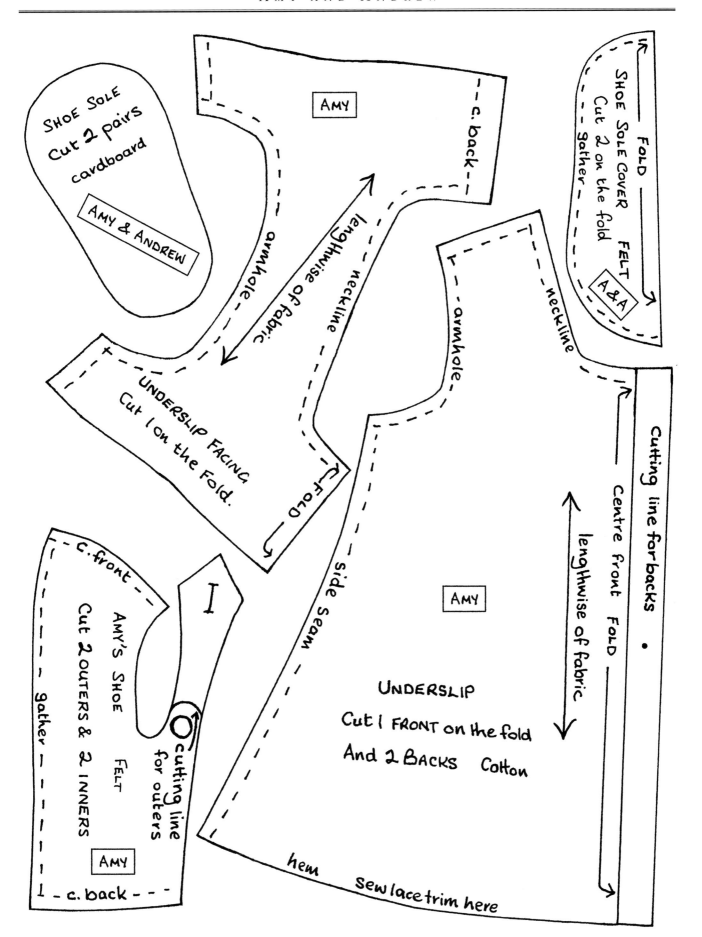

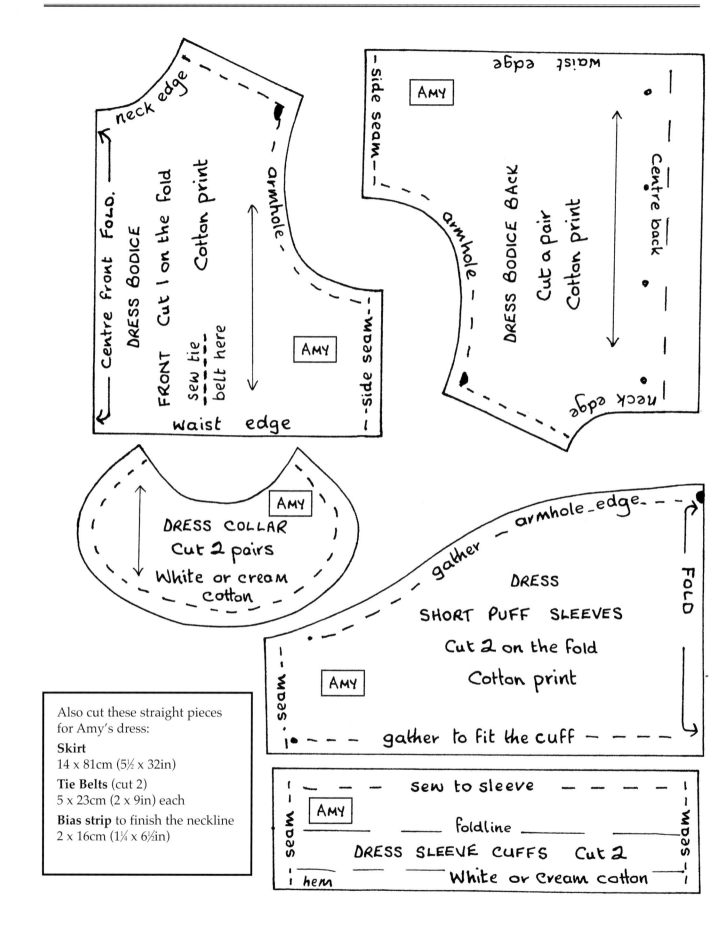

neck edge

Centre Front Fold.

DRESS BODICE

FRONT   Cut 1 on the fold

Cotton print

armhole

sew tie
belt here

AMY

side seam

waist   edge

side seam

waist   edge

AMY

Side seam

armhole

DRESS BODICE BACK

Cut a pair
Cotton print

centre back

neck edge

DRESS COLLAR

Cut 2 pairs

White or cream
cotton

AMY

gather   armhole edge

DRESS

SHORT   PUFF   SLEEVES

Cut 2 on the fold

Cotton print

FOLD

seam

AMY

gather to fit the cuff

sew to sleeve

seam

AMY

foldline

DRESS SLEEVE CUFFS   Cut 2

White or cream cotton

hem

seam

Also cut these straight pieces
for Amy's dress:

Skirt
14 x 81cm (5½ x 32in)

Tie Belts (cut 2)
5 x 23cm (2 x 9in) each

Bias strip to finish the neckline
2 x 16cm (1¼ x 6½in)

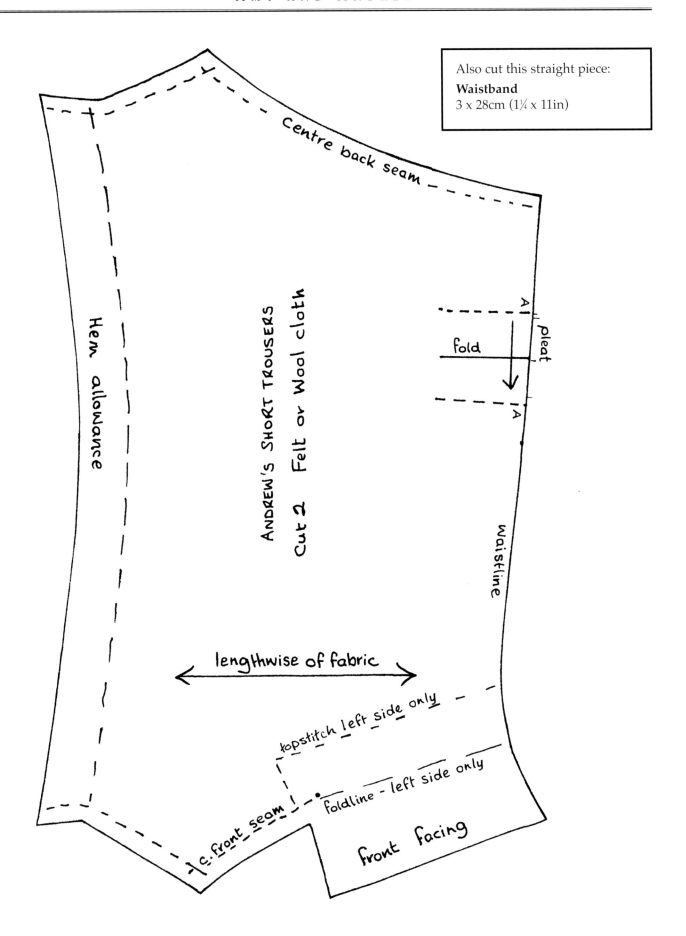

Also cut this straight piece:
Waistband
3 x 28cm (1¼ x 11in)

Centre back seam

Hem allowance

ANDREW'S SHORT TROUSERS
Cut 2 Felt or Wool cloth

fold

pleat

A

A

waistline

lengthwise of fabric

topstitch left side only

foldline - left side only

c. front seam

front facing

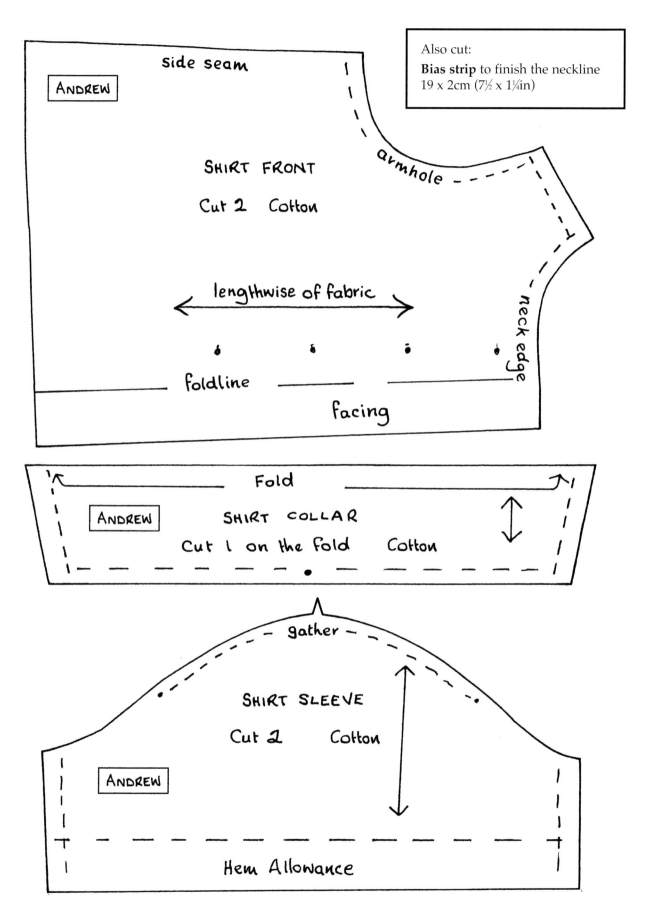

side seam

ANDREW

SHIRT FRONT

Cut 2   Cotton

armhole

lengthwise of fabric

neck edge

foldline

facing

Also cut:
Bias strip to finish the neckline
19 x 2cm (7½ x 1¼in)

Fold

ANDREW   SHIRT COLLAR

Cut 1 on the fold   Cotton

gather

SHIRT SLEEVE

Cut 2   Cotton

ANDREW

Hem Allowance

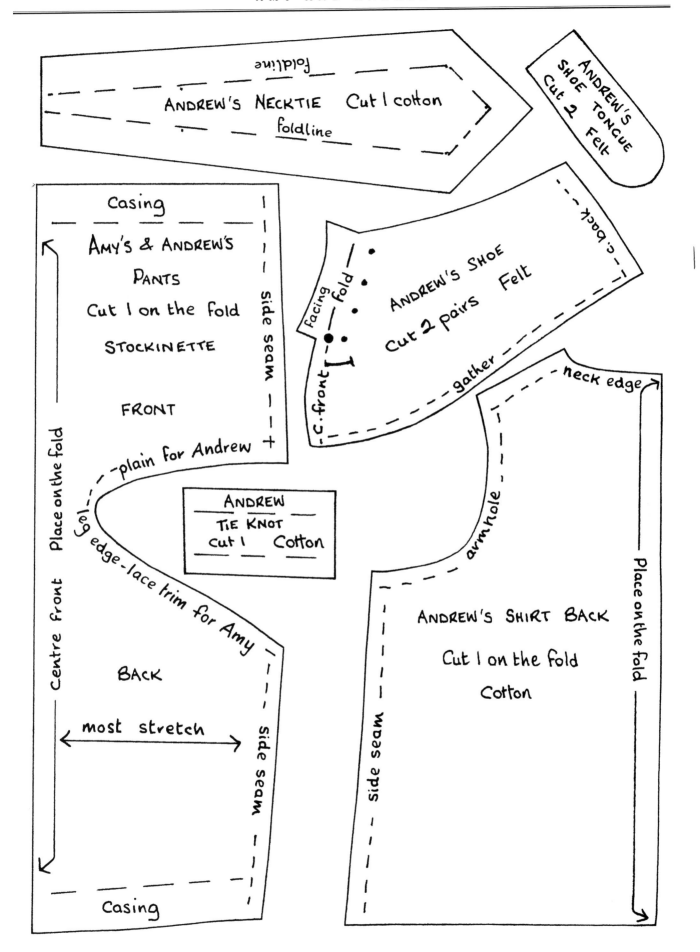

Cassie Marie

Cassie Marie is a 42cm (16½in) calico doll with an old-fashioned rag-doll look and a butter-wouldn't-melt-in-my-mouth expression. She will make a perfect gift for doll-lovers of all ages. The little heart-shaped pocket matches the motif on the bodice of her pinafore.

Materials and equipment

- Unbleached or tinted calico
- Striped, non-stretch cotton (to represent stockings)
- Felt (for the boots); felt in a contrasting colour (for the soles)
- Mohair or other fluffy knitting yarn
- White polyester toy filling
- Stuffing sticks
- Black and brown permanent markers with fine tips; white craft paint; cosmetic blusher
- Thin card to make templates of pattern pieces
- Strong cardboard
- Hot-glue gun (optional)
- Tacky glue
- Cotton tape
- Basic sewing kit, including strong thread, embroidery threads and threads to match all fabrics (including those for the clothes)

Clothes

Underclothes White or cream-coloured cotton or polycotton; broderie anglaise trim, 2.5cm (1in) wide; narrow elastic

Dress 45 x 114cm (18 x 45in) cotton print fabric; snap fasteners

Pinafore and hat brim 60 x 60cm (24 x 24in) felt; snap fasteners or small buttons

Hat crown 30 x 30cm (12 x12in) felt (there will be enough left over to make a pair of boots)

Read *Making the Dolls* on pages 8–11 before you begin.

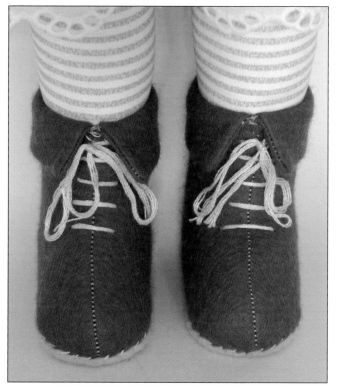

The heart-shaped pocket, which matches the motif on Cassie's pinafore bodice. Both are made by the sew-and-cut method.

Cassie's neat little boots are an integral part of her legs, and are much easier to make than they look.

1 With R.S. facing, sew centre-front seam of body front.

2 Open out, finger press seam and stay-stitch neck edge. Lay body front aside.

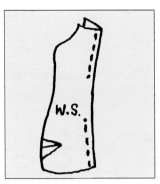

3 With R.S. facing, sew centre-back seam of body back, leaving open between dots. Sew hip darts.

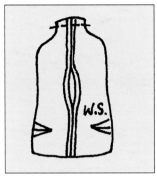

4 Open out body back and stay-stitch neck edge. Lay body back aside.

5 With R.S. facing, sew centre-front seams of boots.

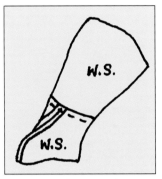

6 Open out boots and sew to legs at ankle edges.

7 Sew centre-back seam of leg and boot.

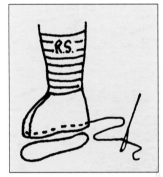

8 Turn legs R.S. out, gather lower edges of boots and insert cardboard soles.

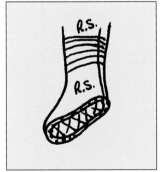

9 Pull up the gathers just enough to hold the inner soles in place. Work a few cross threads over the soles.

10 Gather all round the felt sole covers, insert the second pair of cardboard soles and pull up the gathers to cover.

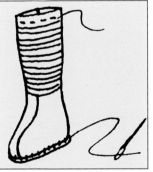

11 Stuff the boots and legs to within 2cm (¾in) of the tops. Line up centre back and front. Tack tops closed and ladder-stitch soles in place.

12 Fold boot collars in half lengthwise and sew the two short sides. Trim the corners, turn R.S. out and tack the tops closed.

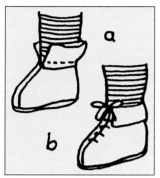

13 Stitch the boot collars in place. Embroider the laces in contrasting thread.

14 Sew legs to body front, leaving the seam allowance free at both sides. After stitching let the legs fall forward.

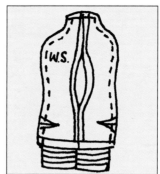

15 With R.S. facing, sew body back to body front at both sides. Turn the body R.S. out.

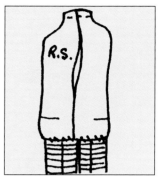

16 Slipstitch lower edge of body and stuff the body through back opening. Close the seam.

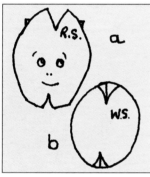

17 Trace the features on the head front. Sew the forehead and chin darts.

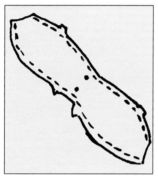

18 Stay-stitch both sides of the head gusset and clip the curved edges to the stay-stitching.

19 With R.S. facing, tack, then sew the head gusset to the head front, matching the notches. Stay-stitch the neck edge.

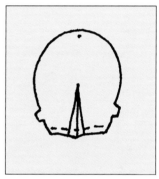

20 Sew the dart in the head back. Stay-stitch the neck edge. With R.S. facing, sew the head back to the head gusset, matching dots and notches.

21 Turn head R.S. out. Stuff firmly. Check that the features are level; if necessary erase and adjust them.

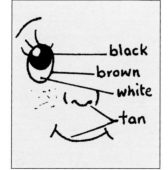

22 Using permanent markers and paint, colour the face and rub the cheeks gently with a cosmetic blusher. Add a few freckles under each eye.

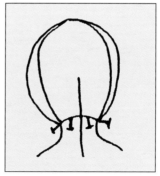

23 Turn in the seam allowance on the neck edge of the body. Pin the head in place. Ladder-stitch the head to the body.

24 Cut about 60 lengths of yarn, each 20cm (8in) long. Do this by winding the yarn around a piece of strong cardboard.

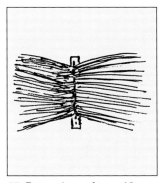

25 Cut a piece of tape 10cm (4in) long, lay the strands of yarn evenly across the tape, leaving 1cm (about ½in) of tape free at each end. Machine through the centre.

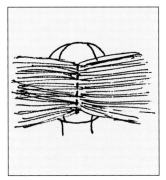

26 Sew or hot-glue the tape to the back of the head, folding under the surplus tape at each end.

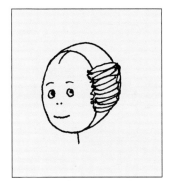

27 Smear the sides of the head with tacky glue. Draw the yarn to each side of the head and backstitch in place. Smear the cut ends with glue.

28 Cut about 70 strands of yarn, each 45cm (18in) long, and stitch to tape 12cm (about 5in) long. Attach to head, as for back, just covering the forehead dart.

29 Stitch the side hair to the head. Plait each side evenly.

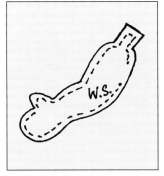

30 With R.S. facing, sew arms together, leaving open between the dots. Clip to stitching at thumb. Turn arms R.S. out.

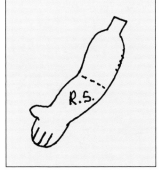

31 Stuff the hands softly and top-stitch the fingers. Stuff lower arm firmly and top-stitch across elbows. Stuff the upper arm softly. Do not stuff the tab. Close the opening.

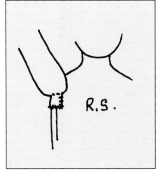

32 Sew the shoulder tab to the underarm area. When the arm hangs the tab will not show.

1 Bloomers. Trim the hems of the legs with broderie anglaise. With R.S. facing, sew centre-front seam.

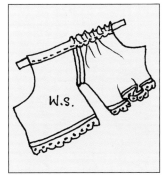

2 Open out, make a casing along the waist edge. Thread with elastic to fit the doll.

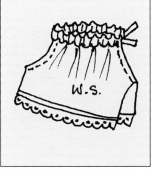

3 Sew the centre-back seam, securing the elastic in the seam.

4 Sew the crotch seam. Turn R.S. out.

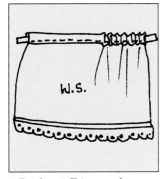

5 Petticoat. Trim one long edge with broderie anglaise. Make a casing along the waist edge and thread with elastic.

6 With R.S. facing, sew the centre-back seam, securing the elastic in the seam.

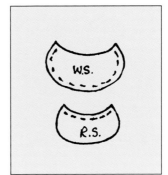

7 Dress. Sew the collars together in pairs and clip the curves to stitching. Turn R.S. out, press and tack openings.

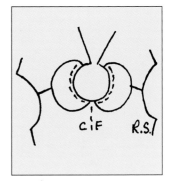

8 With R.S. facing, sew backs to front. Press seams and open out. Sew collars to neck edge, matching centre fronts.

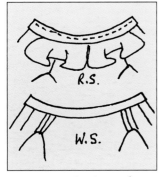

9 Neaten neck edge with bias strip.

10 Press the hem allowance on sleeves to the W.S. Gather the top edges between the dots to fit the armholes.

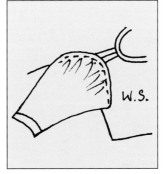

11 With R.S. facing and matching the dots to the shoulder seams, sew the sleeves in place.

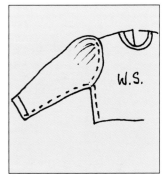

12 With R.S. facing, sew sleeve and side seams.

13 Press the hem allowance of the skirt to the W.S. Gather the waist edge to fit the waist edge of the bodice.

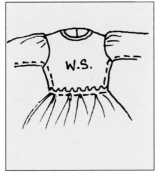

14 With R.S. facing, sew the skirt to the bodice.

15 With R.S. facing, sew the centre-back seam of skirt 10cm (4in) from the hem. Sew snap fasteners to bodice. Hem skirt and sleeves.

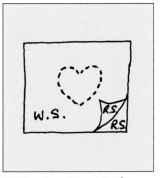

16 Pinafore. To make the pocket and motif, place a scrap of felt on a scrap of dress fabric, R.S. facing. Trace the heart template on one side, machine stitch on the traced line.

17 Cut out the hearts. Make a tiny slit in the felt side to turn through. Turn R.S. out and press.

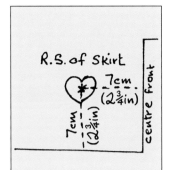

18 Mark the pocket position on the right-hand side of the skirt, 7cm (2 ¾in) up from lower edge and 7cm (2 ¾in) from the centre front. Sew pocket in place, matching *. Sew the motif to bodice front.

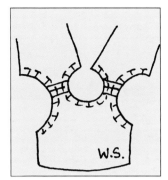

19 With R.S. facing, sew bodice backs to fronts. Press seams. Stay-stitch neck and armhole edges. Clip seam to stitching.

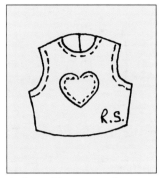

20 Sew side seams of bodice. Turn R.S. out, tack the clipped seam allowance of the neck and armhole edges to W.S. Top-stitch on R.S.

21 Gather the skirt waist to fit the bodice. With R.S. facing, sew skirt in place. Sew snap fasteners to bodice back. Press hem to W.S. and top-stitch on R.S.

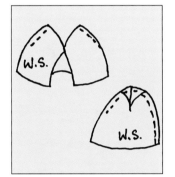

22 Hat. With R.S. facing, sew the two side darts in the hat crown. Sew the front dart, back dart and centre-back seam all in one process. Turn R.S. out and press.

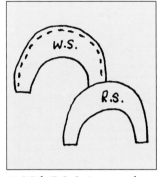

23 With R.S. facing, sew hat brims together along the outer edges. Clip the curves, turn R.S. out and press.

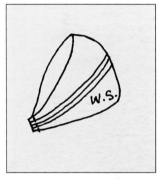

24 Open out and, with R.S. facing, sew centre-back seam of both brims. Press seam flat. Tack inner edges of brims together.

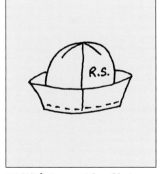

25 With inner side of brim facing R.S. of crown, sew the brim in place, matching the centre-back seams.

26 Press the seam to the inside.

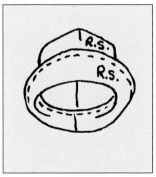

27 Top-stitch the hat brim. The crown may need a little stuffing to give it shape.

28 The hat, which should be very close fitting, should be pulled well down on the doll's head.

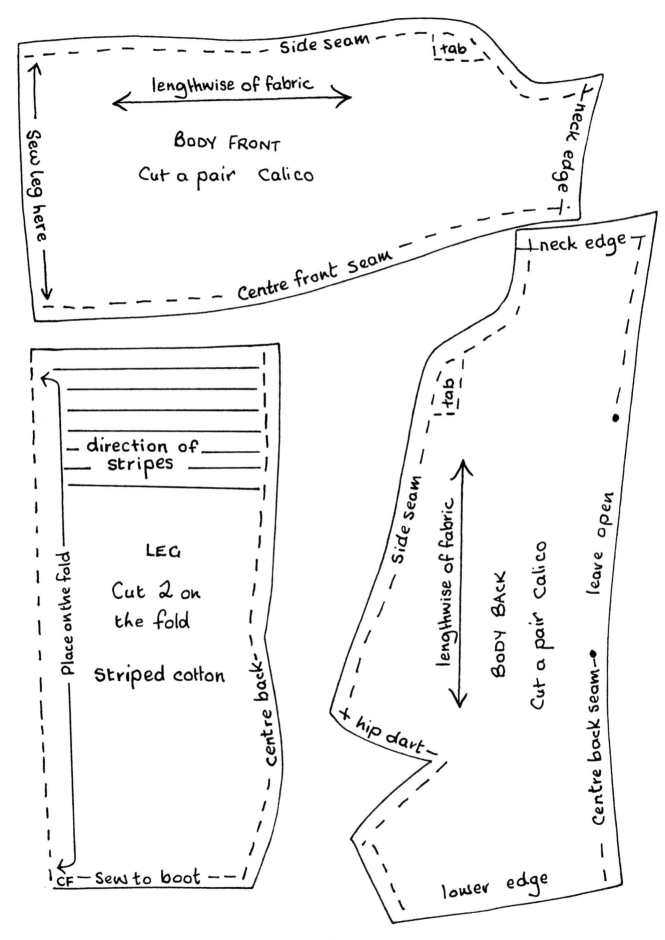

Side seam - - - - - tab

lengthwise of fabric

neck edge

BODY FRONT

Cut a pair Calico

Sew leg here

Centre front Seam - - -

neck edge

direction of stripes

tab

Side seam

lengthwise of fabric

BODY BACK

Cut a pair Calico

leave open

Place on the fold

LEG

Cut 2 on the fold

Striped cotton

centre back

+ hip dart -

Centre back seam -

CF — Sew to boot - - -

lower edge

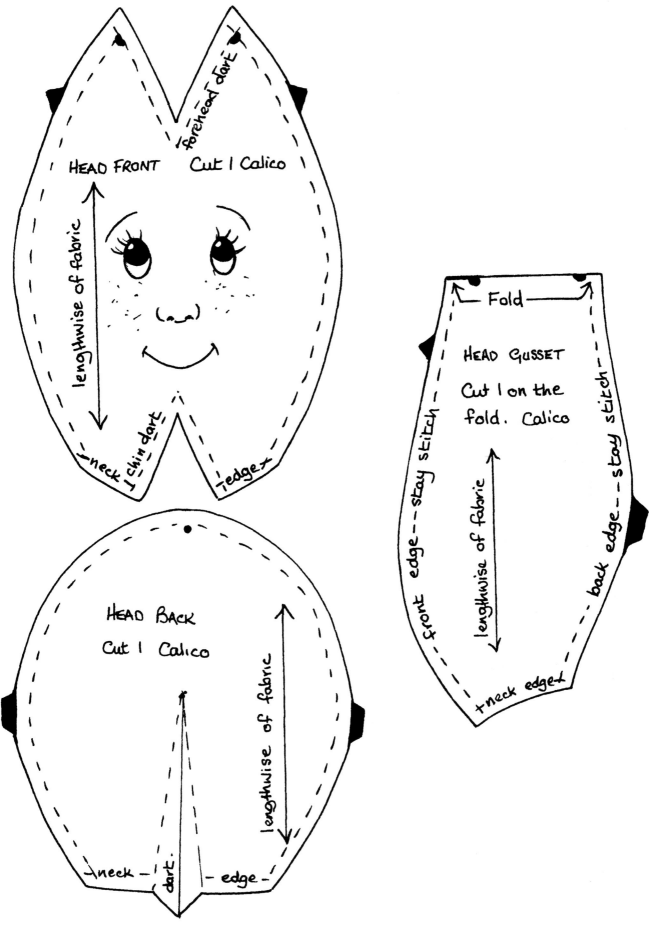

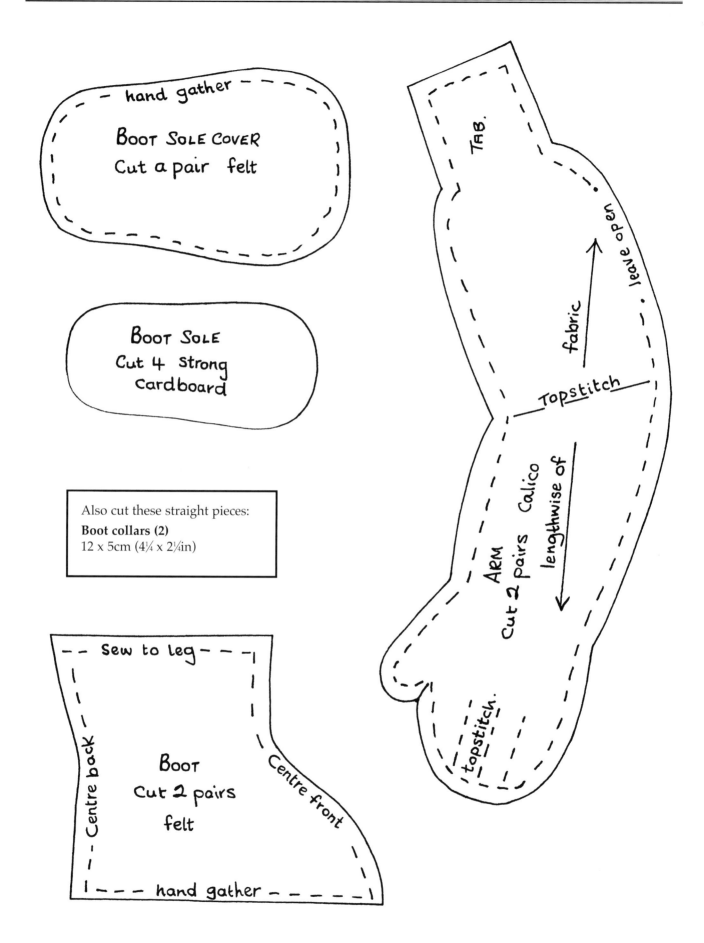

hand gather

BOOT SOLE COVER
Cut a pair felt

BOOT SOLE
Cut 4 strong
cardboard

Also cut these straight pieces:
Boot collars (2)
12 x 5cm (4¼ x 2⅛in)

TAB.

leave open

fabric

Topstitch

ARM
Cut 2 pairs Calico lengthwise of

topstitch.

sew to leg

Centre back

Centre front

BOOT
Cut 2 pairs
felt

hand gather

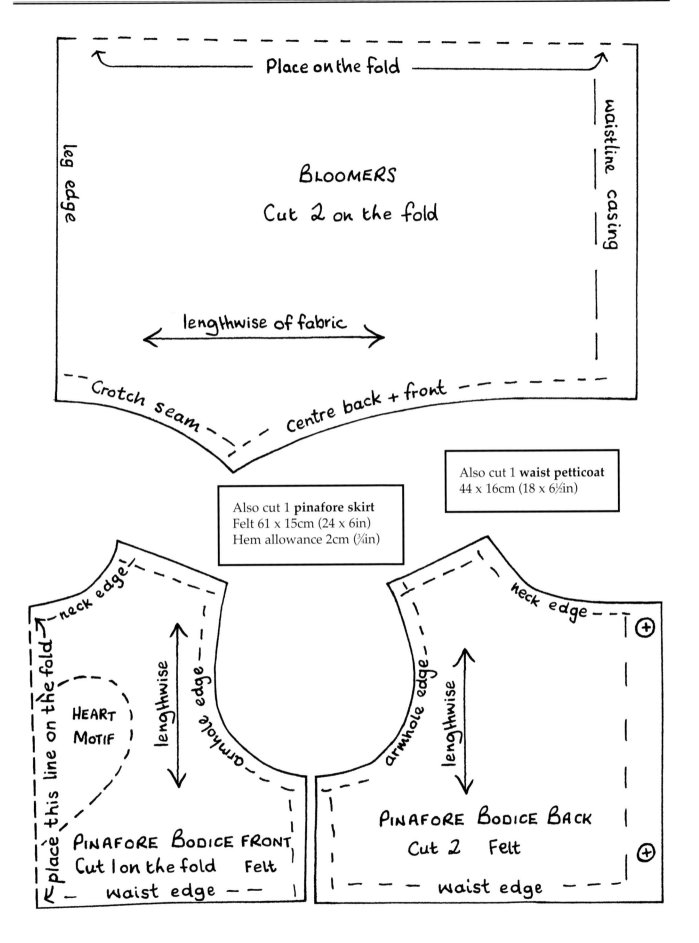

Place on the fold

leg edge

waistline casing

BLOOMERS
Cut 2 on the fold

lengthwise of fabric

Crotch seam

centre back + front

Also cut 1 **waist petticoat**
44 x 16cm (18 x 6½in)

Also cut 1 **pinafore skirt**
Felt 61 x 15cm (24 x 6in)
Hem allowance 2cm (¾in)

neck edge

place this line on the fold

HEART
Motif

lengthwise

armhole edge

PINAFORE BODICE FRONT
Cut 1 on the fold   Felt

waist edge

neck edge

armhole edge

lengthwise

PINAFORE BODICE BACK
Cut 2   Felt

waist edge

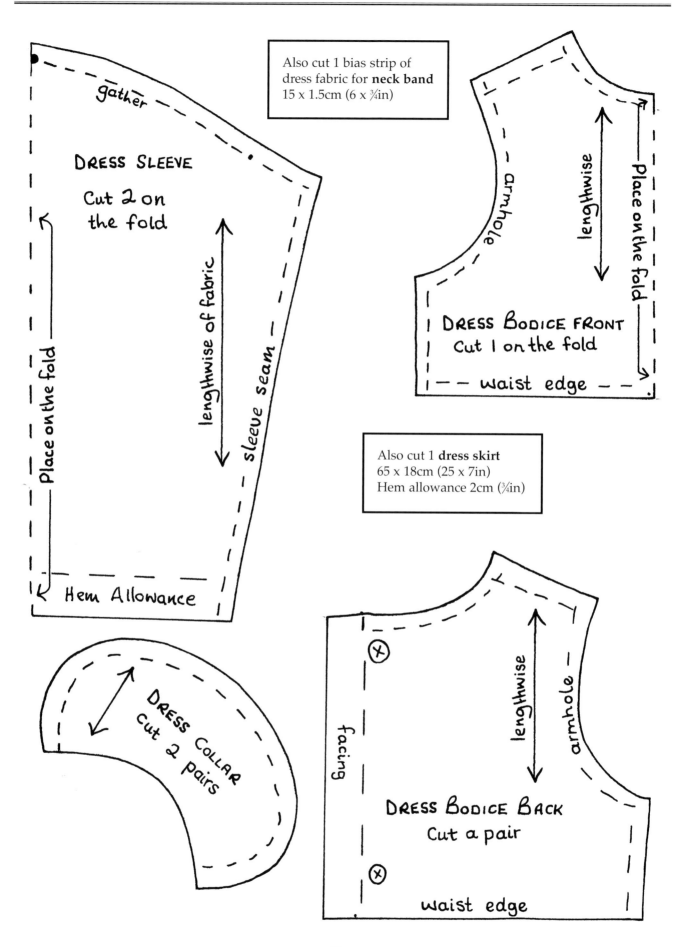

DRESS SLEEVE
Cut 2 on the fold

gather

lengthwise of fabric

sleeve seam

Place on the fold

Hem Allowance

Also cut 1 bias strip of
dress fabric for **neck band**
15 x 1.5cm (6 x ¾in)

DRESS BODICE FRONT
Cut 1 on the fold

armhole

lengthwise

Place on the fold

waist edge

Also cut 1 **dress skirt**
65 x 18cm (25 x 7in)
Hem allowance 2cm (¾in)

DRESS COLLAR
cut 2 pairs

DRESS BODICE BACK
Cut a pair

facing

lengthwise

armhole

waist edge

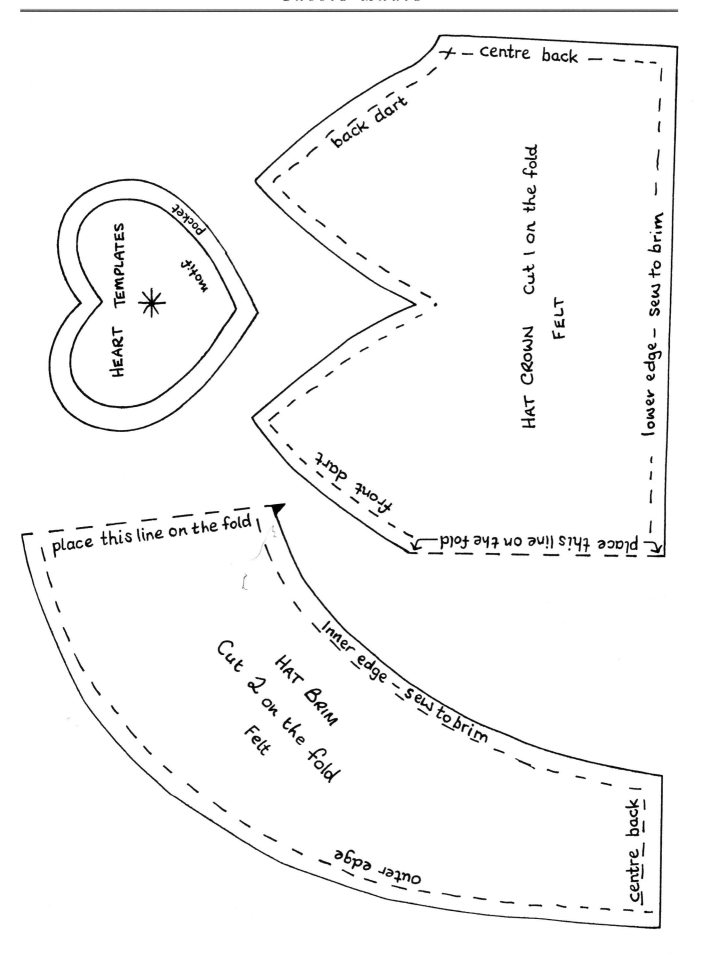

Ruth Anne

Little Ruth Anne is 35cm (14in) high and as bright as the buttons on her winter hat and mittens. Underneath her felt coat she wears a tartan-skirted dress with a T-shirt top. I wonder what she has in her shoulder bag?

Materials and equipment

- Unbleached or tinted calico
- 20 x 20cm (8 x 8in) long fur fabric
- White polyester toy filling
- Stuffing sticks
- Thin card to make templates of pattern pieces
- Black and brown permanent markers with fine tips; white craft paint; soft coral pink crayon pencil
- Basic sewing kit, including strong thread and threads to match all fabrics (including those for the clothes)

Clothes

Knickers and T-shirt top White or cream-coloured T-shirt cotton; narrow elastic; 3 snap fasteners

Dress skirt 10 x 60cm (4 x 24in) thin tartan or checked cotton

Coat 60 x 60cm (24 x 24in) felt; 3 snap fasteners; 3 decorative buttons; top-stitching thread in a contrasting colour

Hat, scarf and mittens 22 x 114cm (8½ x 45in) fleece fabric with a little stretch one way; about 10 small, interesting buttons – e.g., hearts, flowers and other shapes

Shoes and shoulder bag 30 x 30cm (12 x 12in) felt in contrasting colour to the coat; small piece of cotton fabric to line the shoes; beige felt and strong cardboard (for the soles); 2 small shoe buttons; button for the bag

Stockings Pair of white or cream-coloured child's socks

Read *Making the Dolls* on pages 8–11 before you begin.

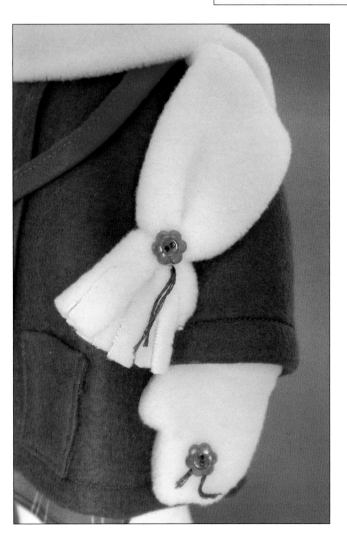

Making the doll
Follow the instructions for Amy and Andrew (see pages 14–17), but with the following differences:
1. Ruth Anne's legs are cut on a fold and therefore have no centre-front seam.
2. The arms are tab-style (like Cassie Marie's) and not jointed.
3. The fur fabric wig should be brushed and cut into a simple basin cut.

Making the clothes
Knickers – follow the instructions for Andrew's pants (without lace).

For all other clothes follow the step-by-step instructions and diagrams on the following pages.

Collect a few interesting buttons and use them to trim Ruth Anne's mittens and scarf to match her hat.

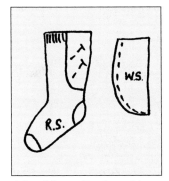

1 Stockings. Cut 2 stockings from the child's socks, using the tops as the open edge. Sew the back seams with a stretch-stitch. Turn R.S. out.

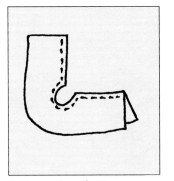

2 Shoes. Sew the lining to the tops along the ankle edges, trim seams and clip curves. Turn R.S. out and press.

3 Open out and sew centre-back seams of shoe and lining. Finger press the seam flat. With W.S. facing, gather lower edge of shoe and lining.

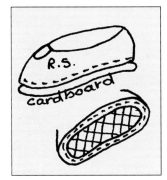

4 Insert cardboard sole in shoe and pull up gathers just enough to hold it in place. Work a few cross threads over the sole.

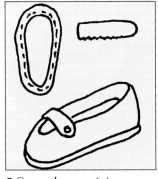

5 Cover the remaining cardboard soles in beige felt. Stitch soles to shoes. Oversew the straps, adjust length to fit the doll, stitch to shoe and sew on snap fastener and button.

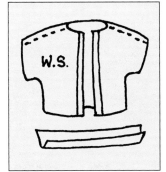

6 T-shirt dress. With R.S. facing, sew backs to front at shoulders. Press centre-back facings to W.S. Press seam allowance on one long edge of neckband to W.S.

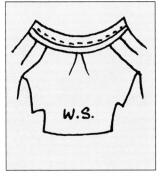

7 With R.S. of neckband facing W.S. of T-shirt, sew neckband in place.

8 Fold neckband with R.S. facing. Sew across both ends at centre back.

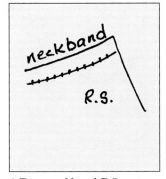

9 Turn neckband R.S. out. Hem in place over the neck seam.

10 Hem the sleeves, sew the side seams and turn the T-shirt top R.S. out. Do not hem.

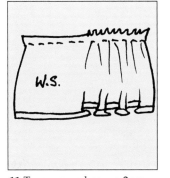

11 Turn up and sew a 2cm (¾in) hem on one long edge of the skirt. Gather the remaining long edge to fit the waist of the T-shirt top without stretching it. Sew the skirt to the top.

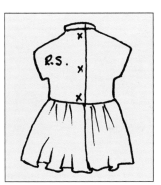

12 Sew the centre back of the skirt for 4cm (1½in) from the hem. Sew snap fasteners to the back opening. Turn the T-shirt dress R.S. out.

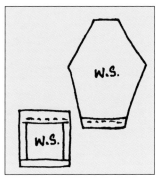

13 Coat. Press the hem allowances of coat sleeves and pockets to the W.S. Using contrasting thread, top-stitch the hems of the sleeves and the tops of the pockets.

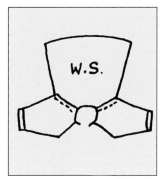

14 With R.S. facing, sew the sleeves to the coat back, matching A–B.

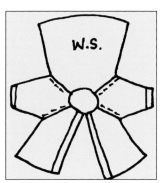

15 With R.S. facing, sew the coat fronts to the sleeves, matching A–B, as before. Press front facings to W.S.

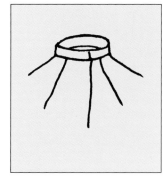

16 Refer to the T-shirt dress for attaching the neckband.

17 With R.S. facing, sew the side seams. Press the hem allowance to the W.S.

18 Turn coat R.S. out. Using contrast thread, top-stitch the hem and front edges and sew on the pockets. Sew on snap fasteners and buttons.

19 Mittens. Hem the wrist edges. Fold with R.S. facing, sew seams and clip to seam at thumb. Turn R.S. out. Sew a button to the back of each mitten, leaving a long thread.

20 Scarf. Fold the scarf strip lengthwise, sew seam and turn R.S. out. Position seam at centre back. Cut both ends into fringes. Using embroidery thread, gather just above fringes. Sew on buttons, leaving long threads.

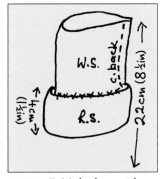

21 Hat. Fold the hat, with R.S. facing, and sew the centre-back seam. Turn 4cm (1½in) hem to W.S. and sew with stretch-stitch or hem loosely.

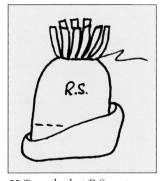

22 Turn the hat R.S. out. Gather tightly 5cm (2in) from the top and fasten off securely.

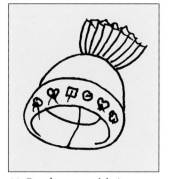

23 Cut the spare fabric at the top into fringes. Using embroidery thread, sew a row of different buttons to the hat brim, leaving a few long threads.

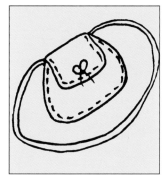

24 Bag. Fold bag with W.S. facing. Use contrasting thread to top-stitch bag and open flap. Fold strap lengthwise and top-stitch seam on R.S. Trim strap and sew in place. Stuff bag lightly. Fold over flap and sew on button.

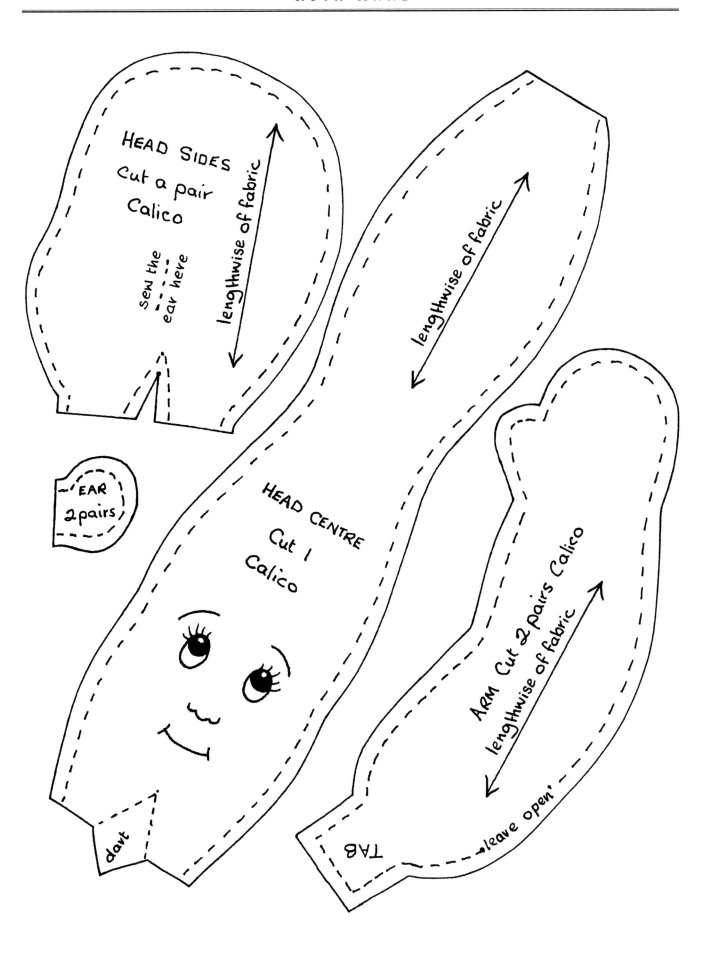

HEAD SIDES
Cut a pair
Calico

sew the
ear here

lengthwise of fabric

lengthwise of fabric

EAR
2 pairs

HEAD CENTRE
Cut 1
Calico

ARM Cut 2 pairs Calico
lengthwise of fabric

dart

TAB

leave open

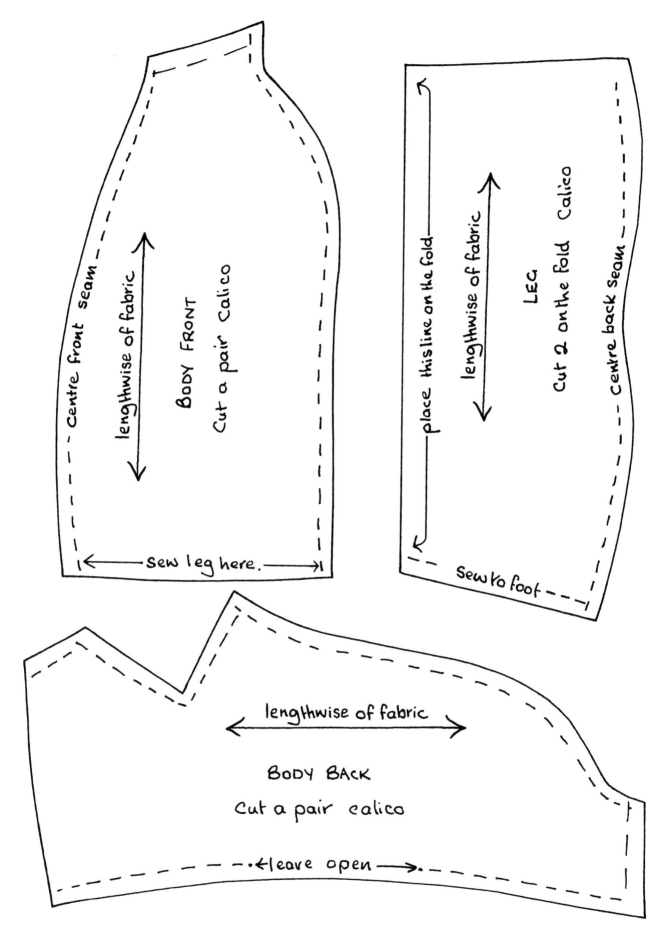

Centre front seam

lengthwise of fabric

BODY FRONT

Cut a pair Calico

sew leg here.

place this line on the fold

lengthwise of fabric

LEG

Cut 2 on the fold Calico

centre back seam

sew to foot

lengthwise of fabric

BODY BACK

Cut a pair calico

leave open

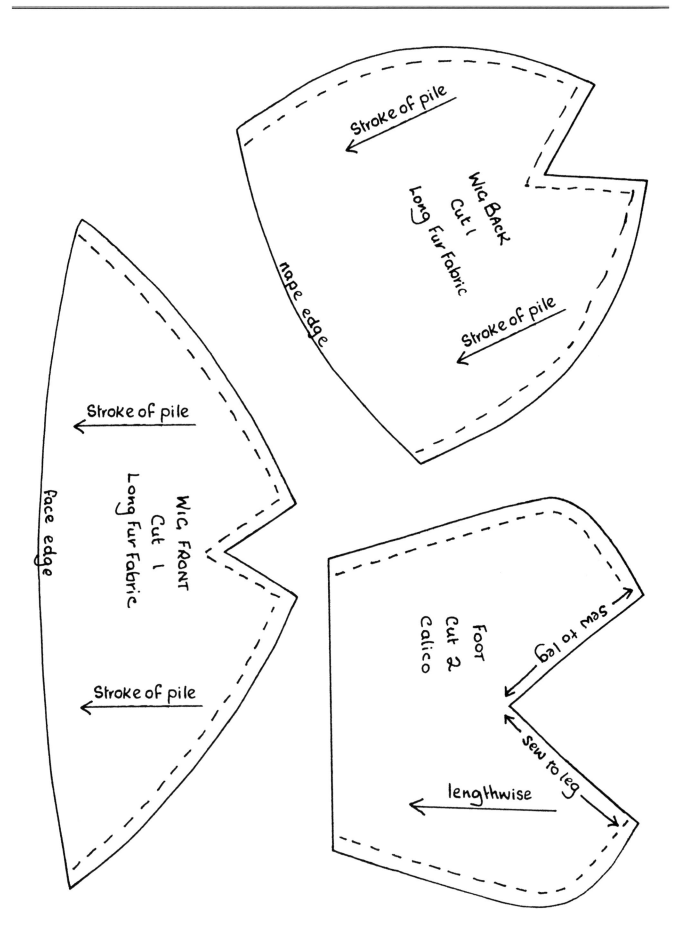

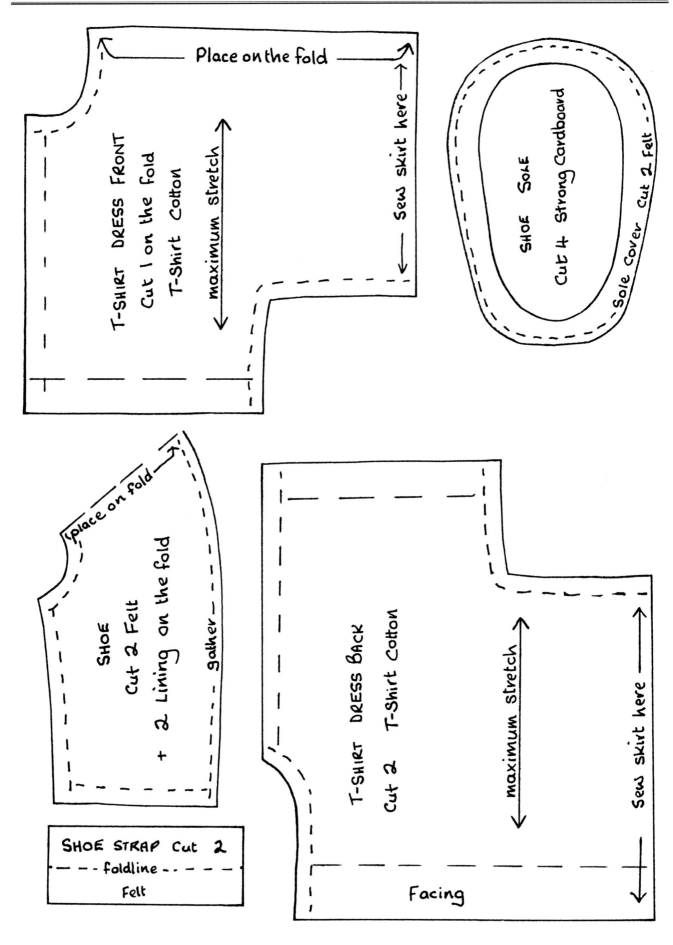

Place on the fold

T-SHIRT DRESS FRONT
Cut 1 on the Fold
T-Shirt Cotton

maximum stretch

Sew skirt here

SHOE SOLE
Cut 4 Strong Cardboard

Sole Cover Cut 2 Felt

place on fold

SHOE
Cut 2 Felt
+ 2 Lining on the fold

gather

T-SHIRT DRESS BACK
Cut 2 T-Shirt Cotton

maximum stretch

Sew skirt here

SHOE STRAP Cut 2
- - - foldline - - -
Felt

Facing

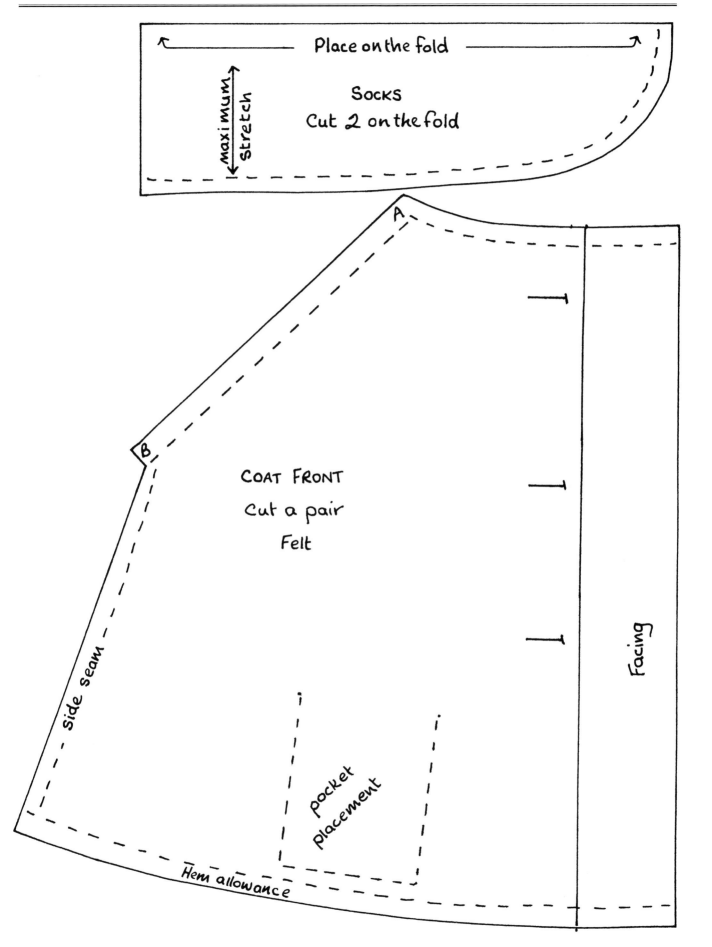

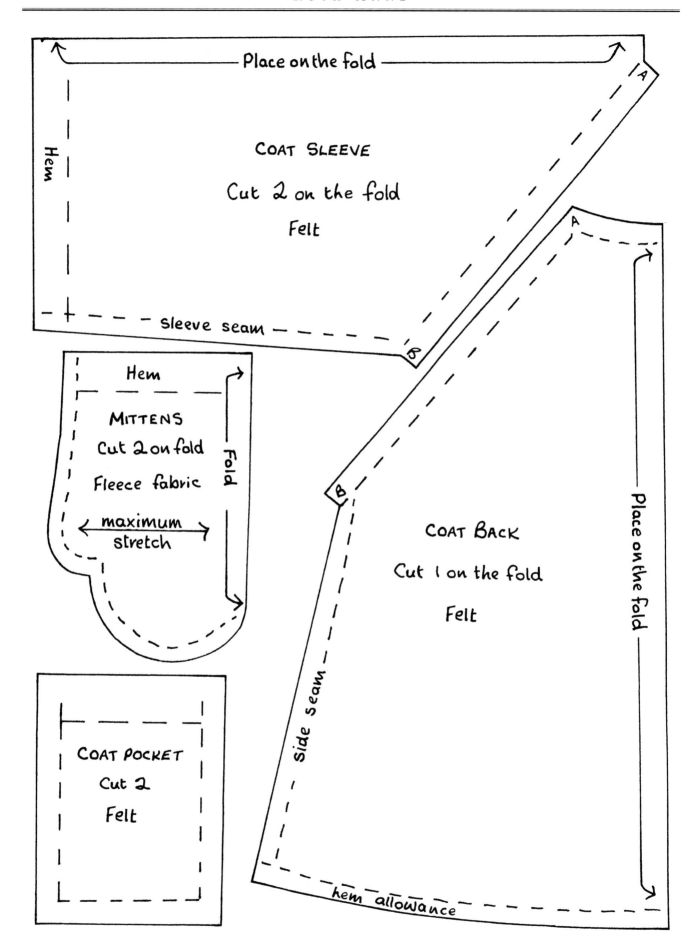

Place on the fold

Hem

COAT SLEEVE

Cut 2 on the fold

Felt

A

A

sleeve seam

B

B

Hem

MITTENS
Cut 2 on fold
Fleece fabric

maximum
stretch

Fold

Place on the fold

COAT BACK

Cut 1 on the fold

Felt

side seam

COAT POCKET
Cut 2
Felt

hem allowance

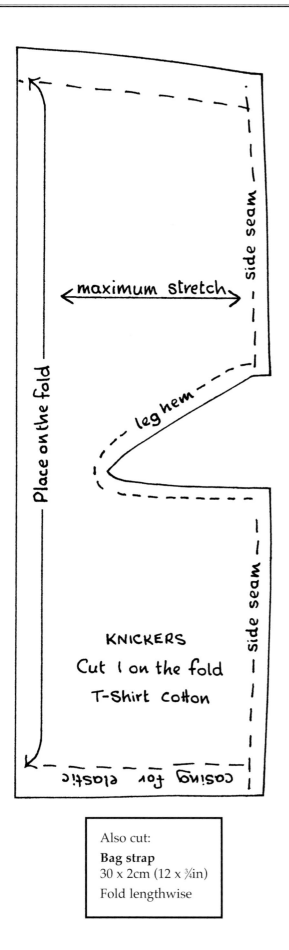

maximum stretch

side seam

Place on the fold

leg hem

side seam

KNICKERS
Cut 1 on the fold
T-Shirt cotton

casing for elastic

Also cut these straight pieces:

Skirt
10 x 60cm (4 x 24in)

Hat
22 x 29cm (9 x 11in), maximum stretch across 29cm (11in) width; cut from fleece fabric

Scarf
9 x 50cm (3½ x 16in), maximum stretch across 9cm (3½in) width; cut from fleece fabric

Coat neckband
5 x 20cm (2 x 8in)

T-shirt top neckband
3 x 18cm (1¼ x 7in)

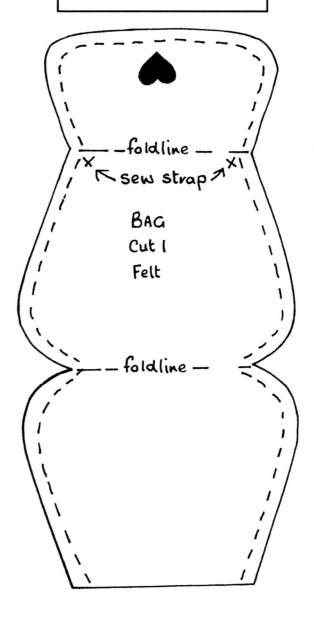

foldline

X   sew strap   X

BAG
Cut 1
Felt

foldline

Also cut:

Bag strap
30 x 2cm (12 x ¾in)
Fold lengthwise

Covered Needlesculpture

A porcelain doll artist sculpts the original head in clay from which a mould is made. Covered needle-sculpture dolls are sculpted in cloth, often using several different weaves and textures to achieve the desired result. Each one is a true original as no moulds or masks are made from them.

The Head

The contours of the face are built by stitching or gluing pads of fabric and stuffing onto a stuffed head base. The padded head is then covered in a stretchy 'skin' and the features are painted. The face can be further enhanced by a little needle modelling and shading. The most suitable fabric for covering the head is cotton stockinette, which clings to the fabric underneath and is easy to glue and to paint. After painting it can be sealed with a clear matt sealer such as 'Mod Podge' if desired. Ginger's face has been sealed in this way.

If you are adapting an existing pattern the head must always be made slightly smaller to allow for the padding.

The Body

Calico bodies are quite suitable, especially if the calico is tinted to match the stockinette head. Bodies can be made of stockinette too, but it must be stabilised first by backing with a woven iron-on interfacing; non-woven interfacings are not suitable as they tear at the seams during stuffing because the machine needle has perforated them during sewing. Ginger's body is made from interface-lined stockinette.

Hints and Tips

Study the diagrams carefully before you begin. As you will see, the features are made from little 'cushions'. When you gather the circles of stockinette to make the cushions use tiny gathering stitches and keep them as close to the edge as possible. Remember: before cutting, the most stretch of the fabric must go across the nose piece.

The nose needs to be stuffed very firmly, and the easiest way to do this is to roll a piece of stuffing into a small ball and place it inside the gathered nose, then

How to sew, turn and stuff small, separate fingers

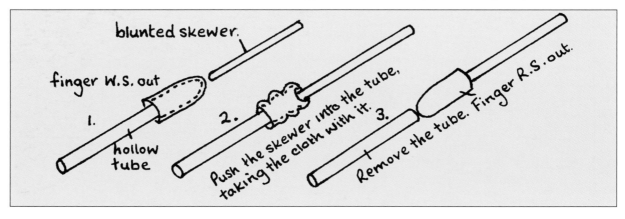

Before you begin, note the 'lengthwise of fabric' or 'maximum stretch' arrows on the pattern piece. Calico hands will be laid on the bias to make turning easier. The hand pattern is usually a template. Cut it out carefully in card, lay it on the double fabric and draw round it lightly with a fine pink or tan marker. Sew the hand right on the line, using very small machine stitches, and sew the rest of the arm as usual. If the pattern has darts on the insides of the wrist, make sure you have a right and a left arm and sew them now. Trim the fabric around the fingers closely, snipping into the V-shapes between the fingers.

To turn the fingers right side out you will need a hollow tube such as a hollow plastic lollipop stick, a length of tube from a spray detergent bottle or even a plastic drinking straw – and a blunt stick, like a barbecue skewer. Follow the diagrams above.

After turning the fingers, stuff them by twirling a wisp of stuffing around the pointed end of a barbecue skewer and pushing it right into the end of each finger. Twist the skewer in the opposite direction to release it, while holding the stuffing in place with your other hand. If the second and third fingers are joined, topstitch between them.

pull up the gathers tightly. Try to keep the triangular shape of the nose as you work. You will find this easier if you begin and end the gathers at the bridge (top) of the nose and pin that point in place before stitching it to the face.

The cheeks and chin need to be stuffed very softly. Pull up the gathering stitches pulled up just enough to hold the stuffing; if they are stuffed too firmly they will have hard edges, which will show under the covering. Place and pin both cheeks to the head base before stitching to make sure they are even. Stitch all round them with tiny

ladder-stitches. You may need to go round twice to keep the edges soft and flat.

Do not place the chin cushion too high. Remember the chin is at the tip of the face, so leave sufficient room for the mouth. There may be times when a particular doll needs a little padding on the forehead, too.

The area between the nose and chin usually needs to be raised a little. Cut out shapes to fit from felt scraps and glue them in place. Lips may be cut from felt and glued in place, too. Often a painted mouth on the finished head is all that is necessary.

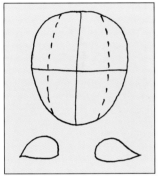

1 Make up the head as for a basic calico doll and stuff firmly. Using contrasting thread, divide the face into quarters. Make a pair of eye templates from thin card, using the pattern provided on page 57.

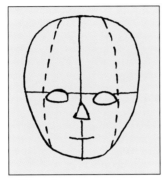

2 Place the eye templates just below the central horizontal line, about an eye's width apart. Draw around them with a sharp pencil.

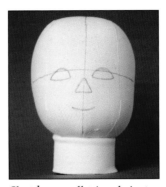

Sketch a small triangle just below the eyes; this is where the nose will be sewn. Draw a short line at the mouth position. Remove the guide threads.

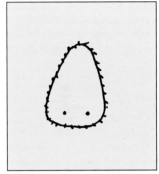

3 Gather all round the nose, keeping to the very edge. Stuff firmly and pull up the gathers fully. Sew the nose to the face with tiny ladder-stitches, keeping to the triangular shape. Mark the nostrils.

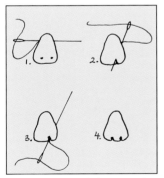

4 Needle-model the nostrils following the diagrams.

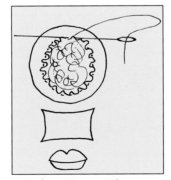

5 Gather all round the cheeks and chin, keeping to the very edges, and pull up the gathers a little. Stuff the circles very softly so that they do not leave hard edges when sewn to the face. Cut out felt shapes to fill the area between the nose and chin. If wished, also cut out felt lips.

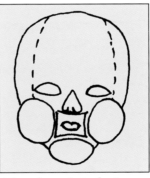

6 Sew the pads to the face, keeping the edges stretched as flat as possible.

Glue on the felt shapes and lips. At this stage the face looks very strange – but don't worry.

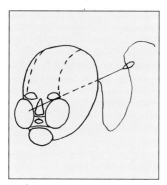

7 Thread a long needle with strong thread and secure the thread at the back of the head. Push the needle through to the outer corner of the right eye.

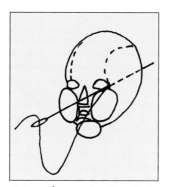

Return the needle almost at the same spot, pull on the thread just enough to indent the eye corner and repeat the stitch. Work the inner corner of the eye in the same way. Repeat with the left eye.

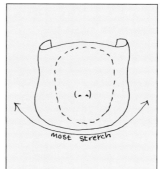

8 Smear tacky white craft glue over the nose and nostrils. Place the head cover centrally over the face, smooth fabric over nose without stretching. Push fabric into the nostrils, holding it in place with two straight pins until dry.

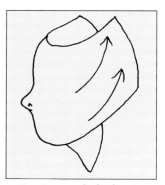

9 Gently stretch the head cover upwards and to the centre back of the head. Do not overstretch the fabric. Trim excess fabric at the centre back.

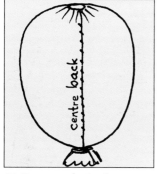

10 Oversew the back seam neatly and tightly gather the excess fabric at the neck.

Trim the top edge and also gather tightly.

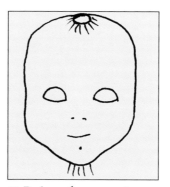

11 Redraw the eyes using the original templates. Indent the eye corners as before. Mark the corners of

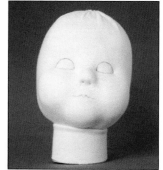

the mouth and indent them as you did the eyes. Dimples in chin or cheeks are made the same way.

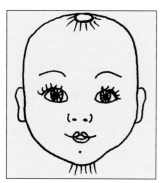

12 Make the ears from scraps of interface-lined stockinette and sew in place.

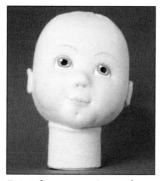

Paint the eyes and mouth following the instructions in the face painting section (see pages 10–11).

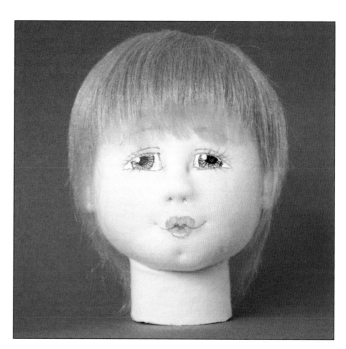

13 The finished head with wig.

Patterns for head and arm with separate fingers
for covered needlesculpture dolls

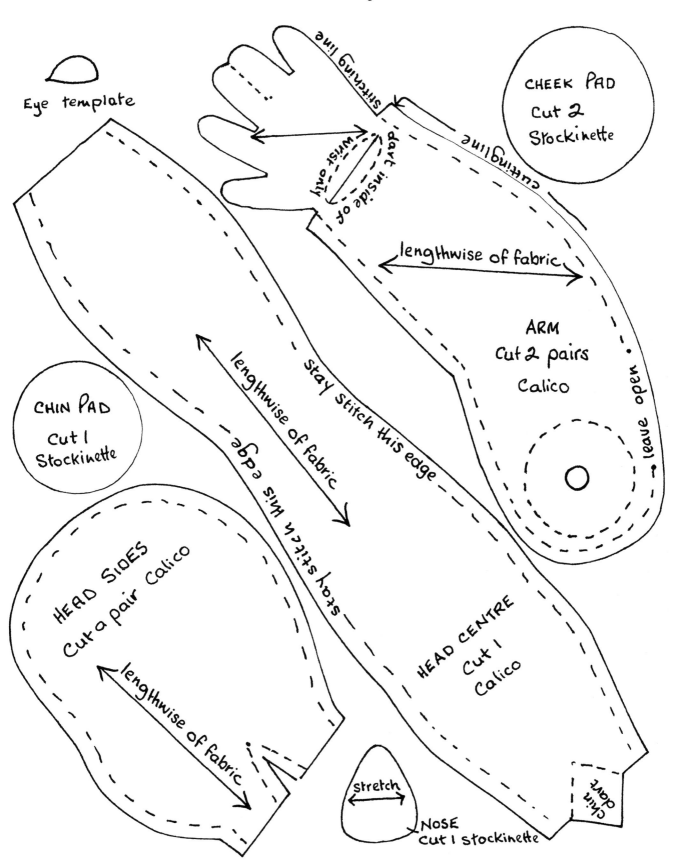

Eye template

CHEEK PAD
Cut 2
Stockinette

stitching line

wrist only

dart inside of

cutting line

lengthwise of fabric

ARM
Cut 2 pairs
Calico

leave open

CHIN PAD
Cut 1
Stockinette

stay stitch this edge

lengthwise of fabric

stay stitch this edge

HEAD SIDES
Cut a pair Calico

HEAD CENTRE
Cut 1
Calico

lengthwise of fabric

chin dart

stretch

NOSE
cut 1 stockinette

David

David, the evacuee boy, stands 39cm (15½in) tall. He represents the many children who, in the early 1940s, were sent from the large towns and cities to the safety of the countryside for the duration of the war. Clutching his new gas mask in its cardboard box, he is trying to be very brave, but it is not easy because he doesn't know where he is going or when he will see his mum and dad again.

Materials and equipment

- Flesh-coloured calico
- Flesh-coloured stockinette
- Scraps of flesh-coloured or white felt
- Set of 3cm (1¼in) plastic joints
- Fur fabric (for the wig)
- Thin card to make templates of pattern pieces
- White polyester toy filling
- Stuffing sticks
- Fabric paints; permanent markers; colour pencils (see face painting, pages 10–11)
- White tacky craft glue
- Basic sewing kit, including strong thread and threads to match all fabrics (including those for the clothes)
- Buff-coloured luggage label

Clothes

Pants Thin stockinette or T-shirt fabric; narrow elastic

Jacket and trousers Plain grey flannel, thin wool tweed or similar; strong snap fastener; 2 small buttons

Cap Felt; cotton for lining; small piece of iron-on interfacing

Shirt Plain cream-coloured or blue cotton; snap fasteners or decorative buttons

Necktie Plain cotton; narrow elastic

Socks Pair of fawn or grey child's socks

Shoes Felt or thin leather; felt in contrasting colour or leather (for soles); strong cardboard; embroidery thread

Gas mask box Thin card; brown paper; about 40cm (16in) thin parcel string

---

Read *Making the Dolls* on pages 8–11
before you begin.

Making the doll

Read through the points on covered needlesculpture and the instructions for making the head before you begin.

Use the pattern for the body and legs of Amy and Andrew, the basic calico dolls, and make up the body and legs in exactly the same way (see page 15). You can also use Andrew's arms or the more realistic ones with separate fingers – both are jointed.

The head

The heads of covered needlesculpture dolls are smaller than those of the basic calico dolls to allow for the extra padding, so make sure you use the correct pattern. Make up the head as Andrew's, except for the ears, which are sewn in place after the head is covered (see page 16). The doll's ears should be made of stockinette to match the texture of the head: make them from a scrap of stockinette backed with iron-on interfacing.

Stuff the head very firmly through the neck opening and work a few cross threads over the opening to keep the stuffing in place. Do not sew the head to the body yet. Cut out the cheek, chin and nose pieces from stockinette – note the direction of the stretch on the nose piece. Cut a head cover 22 x 15cm (8½ x 6in) from stockinette, with most stretch going across the 22cm (8½in) width.

Follow the instructions for making a covered needle-sculpture head (see pages 54–56). When it is complete, sew the head in place.

The hair

Use the pattern and instructions for Andrew's wig and hairstyle (see page 14).

Making the clothes

Make the pants, socks, shirt and tie exactly as Andrew's.

Make the trousers in the same way as Andrew's, but add 1cm (about ½in) to the leg length before cutting out.

The shoes can be made from felt or leather; if you are using leather note the special instructions on page 62.

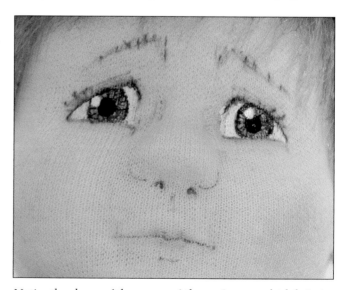

Notice the shape of the eyes and the eyebrows, which help to give David an anxious expression.

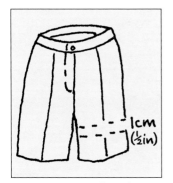

1 Trousers. Lengthen the legs by 1cm (about ½in).

2 Jacket. Fold the pocket flaps in half, R.S. facing. Sew both side seams. Turn R.S. out, tack tops and sew pocket flaps in place. Press down.

3 With R.S. facing, sew the shoulder seams.

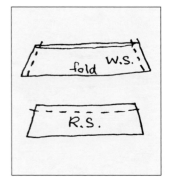

4 Fold the collar with R.S. facing. Sew both end seams. Trim the corners. Turn R.S. out, press and tack openings.

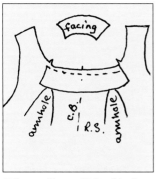

5 Sew collar to R.S. of jacket neckline, matching centre of collar to the centre back of the jacket.

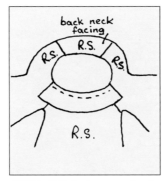

6 With R.S. facing, sew back neck facing to side facings.

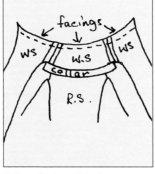

7 Sew facings in place over the collar through all thicknesses.

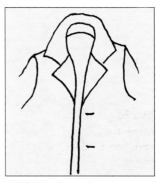

8 Trim seam and corners. Turn R.S. out and press.

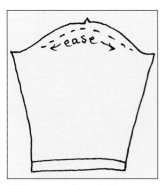

9 Ease top edge of sleeves between dots. Press hem allowance of sleeves to W.S.

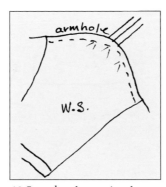

10 Sew the sleeves in place.

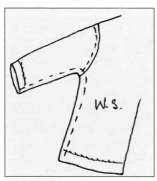

11 Sew the side seams. Hem the sleeves and jacket.

12 Make buttonholes and sew on the buttons.

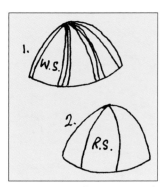

13 Cap. Sew all 6 sections of the cap together, turn R.S. out and press. Make the lining in the same way.

14 Trim the seam allowance from the cap peak interfacing and iron to the W.S. of one cap peak. With R.S. facing, sew peaks together. Trim seam, turn R.S. out and press. Tack opening.

15 Sew the peak to the lower edge of the cap, matching the centre-front notch to the centre of one panel.

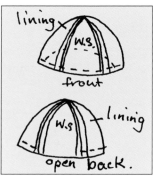

16 With R.S. facing, place the cap lining over cap and peak. Sew together at the lower edge through all thicknesses, leaving an opening at the back.

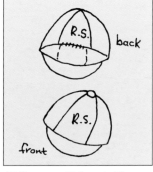

17 Turn cap R.S. out. Close the opening and press. Glue a small felt circle to the crown.

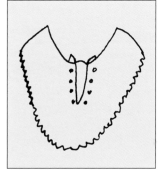

18 Leather shoe. Cut the lower edge with pinking scissors. Cut a shoe sole from thicker leather, using the card sole pattern (see Andrew's shoe, page 23).

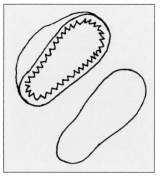

19 Glue the pinked edge to the underside of the cardboard sole.

20 When dry, glue the leather sole in place.

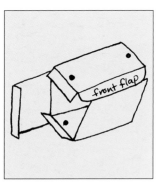

21 Gas mask box. Fold along the perforations. Punch string holes as marked.

22 Glue the box together with the front flap on the outside. Thread the string through the holes.

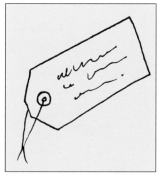

23 Luggage label. Use an ordinary buff-coloured label cut down to size.

24 Write the child's name and destination on it and attach it to the jacket.

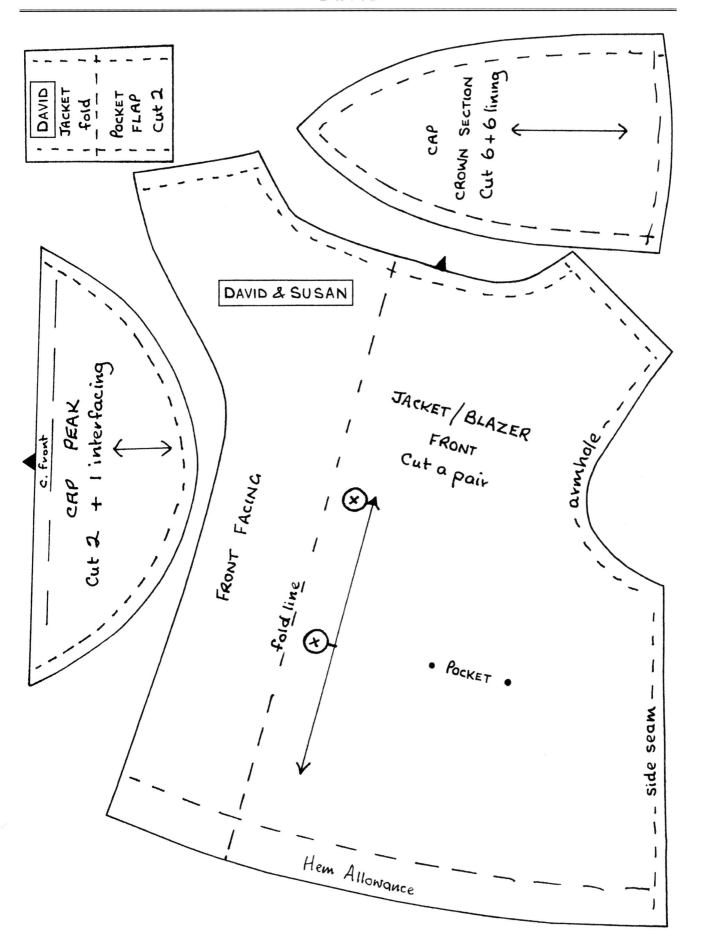

DAVID

JACKET
fold

POCKET
FLAP
Cut 2

CAP
CROWN SECTION
Cut 6 + 6 lining

DAVID & SUSAN

CAP PEAK
Cut 2 + 1 interfacing

c. front

JACKET/BLAZER
FRONT
Cut a pair

armhole

FRONT FACING

fold line

Pocket

side seam

Hem Allowance

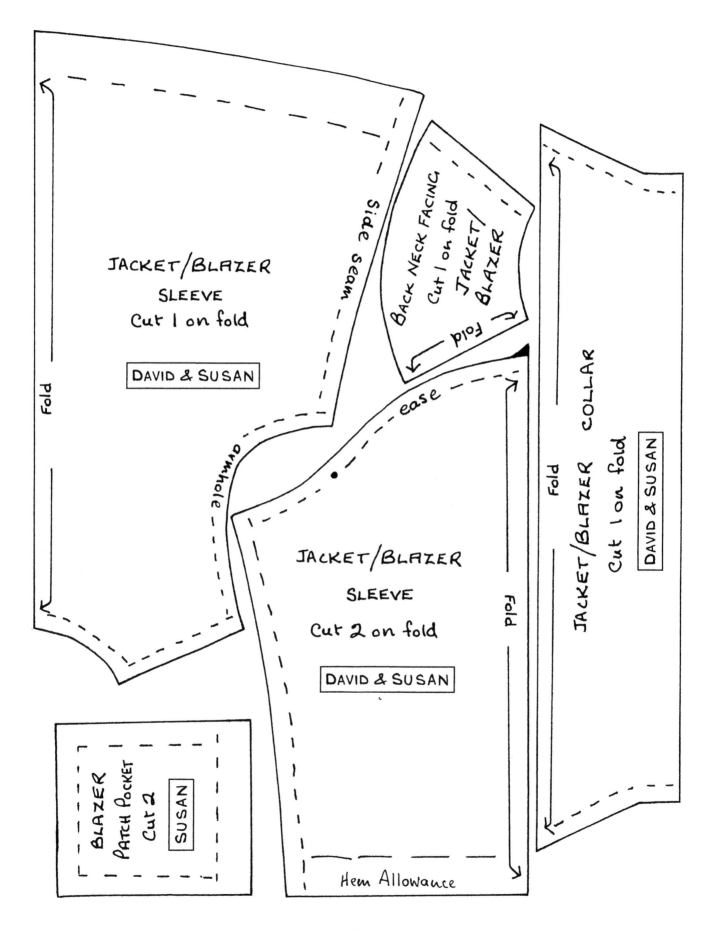

JACKET/BLAZER
SLEEVE
Cut 1 on fold

DAVID & SUSAN

Side seam

BACK NECK FACING
Cut 1 on fold

JACKET/
BLAZER

fold

Fold

ease

armhole

JACKET/BLAZER

SLEEVE

Cut 2 on fold

DAVID & SUSAN

Fold

JACKET/BLAZER COLLAR

Cut 1 on fold

DAVID & SUSAN

Fold

BLAZER
PATCH POCKET
Cut 2

SUSAN

Hem Allowance

David's gas mask box

Cut 1 in thin card covered in brown paper

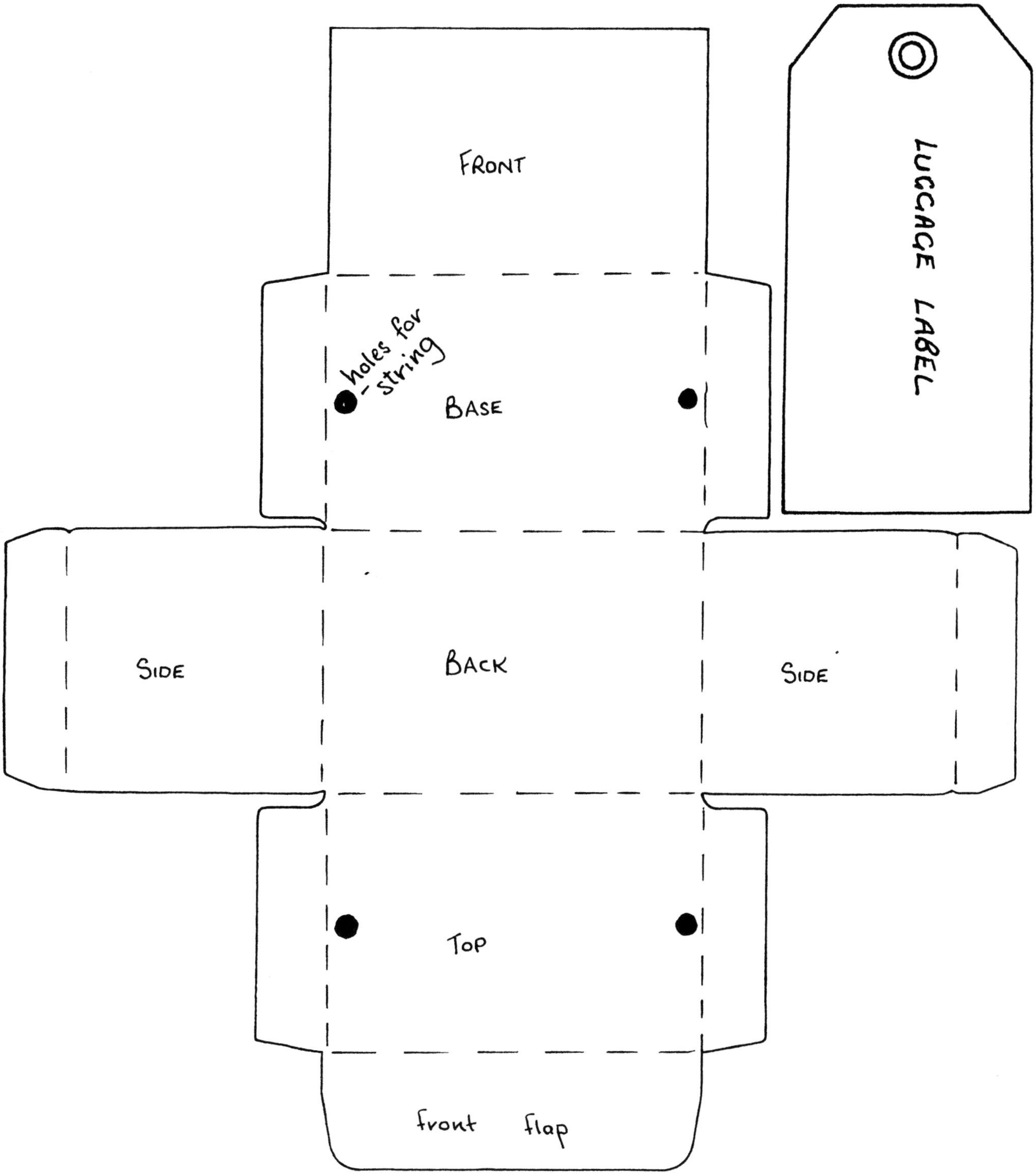

FRONT

holes for string

BASE

LUGGAGE LABEL

SIDE

BACK

SIDE

TOP

front flap

Susan

Susan is 39cm (15½in) tall. A little girl starting a new school, this is the first time she has worn a proper school uniform, and she is very proud of her smart satchel and blazer and hat, with their bright red braid.

Materials and equipment

- Flesh-coloured calico
- Flesh-coloured stockinette
- Scraps of flesh-coloured or white felt
- Set of 3cm (1¼in) plastic joints
- Long fur-fabric (for the wig)
- Narrow ribbon
- Thin card to make templates of pattern pieces
- White polyester toy filling
- Stuffing sticks
- Fabric paints; permanent markers; colour pencils (see face painting, pages 10–11)
- White tacky craft glue
- Basic sewing kit, including strong thread and threads to match all fabrics (including those for the clothes)

Clothes

Pants Thin stockinette; narrow elastic; narrow lace trim

Blazer and hat Navy blue felt; red Russian braid; iron-on interfacing; 2 small buttons

Dress Cotton or polycotton with a small red gingham check; snap fasteners or decorative buttons

Underslip White cotton or polycotton; broderie anglaise trim, 15mm (½in) wide; small button

Shoes Navy blue felt or leather; felt or leather in contrasting colour (for soles); 2 small buttons

Socks Pair of white child's socks

School satchel Tan leather or felt; 2 small buckles

Read *Making the Dolls* on pages 8–11 before you begin.

Russian braid is a fine two-cord braid. To attach it neatly, sew between the cords with matching thread.

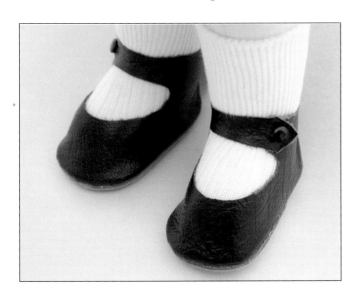

Making the doll
Follow the instructions for making David up to the hair (see page 60).

The hair
Use the pattern for Amy's wig (see page 14). Cut a neat fringe for Susan. Tie the hair back at each side and sew two red hair ribbons in place.

Making the clothes
Make the pants, underslip and socks exactly as Amy's (see pages 17 and 19).

Make the dress as Amy's but do not use contrasting fabric for the collar and cuffs. Omit the tie belt, which will look bulky under the blazer.

The shoes may be made from felt or leather. If you use leather, follow the instructions for David's shoe soles (see page 62).

Make the blazer as David's jacket but add patch pockets. Sew Russian braid to the collar, cuffs and pocket tops.

Susan's leather shoes. Use a soft, pliable leather for the uppers and a heavier one for the soles.

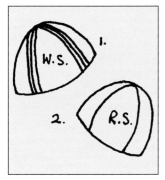

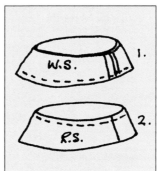

1 School hat. Sew all 5 sections of the crown together. Turn R.S. out and press.

2 Fuse the interfacing to one side of the hat brim. Sew the centre-back seam of both brim sections.

3 With R.S. facing, sew the brim sections together along the outside edge. Trim the seam, turn R.S. out and press.

4 With W.S. of brim facing R.S. of crown, sew the hat brim to the crown. Press seam to inside.

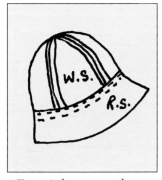

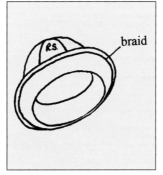

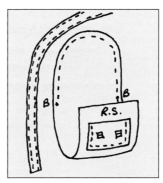

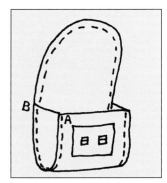

5 Top-stitch seam on the inside.

6 Sew red Russian braid to the outside edge of the hat brim.

7 Satchel. Sew buckles to the satchel pocket. Sew the pocket in place. Top-stitch the flap and shoulder strap.

8 Sew in side panels, matching A–B. Sew the buckle straps and shoulder straps in place.

If tan leather is unavailable Susan's school satchel would look just as smart made from tan felt with darker top-stitching.

The brim of the soft felt school hat is backed with a fusible interfacing to help retain its shape.

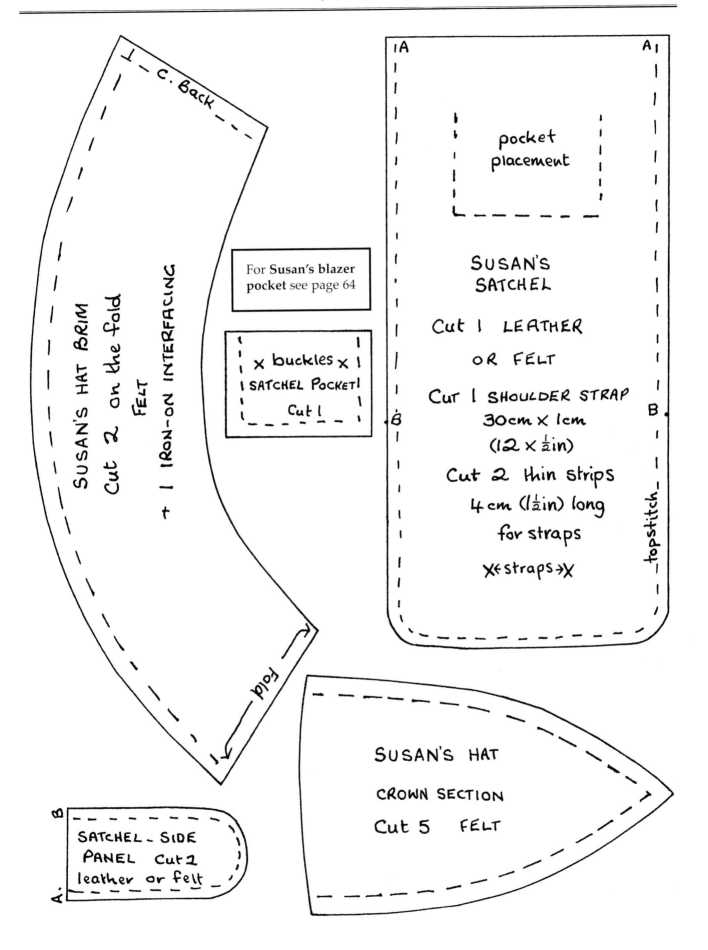

SUSAN'S HAT BRIM

Cut 2 on the fold

FELT

+ 1 IRON-ON INTERFACING

C. Back

Fold

For **Susan's blazer pocket** see page 64

x buckles x
SATCHEL POCKET
Cut 1

A   A

pocket
placement

SUSAN'S
SATCHEL

Cut 1 LEATHER

OR FELT

Cut 1 SHOULDER STRAP
30cm x 1cm
$(12 \times \frac{1}{2}in)$

Cut 2 thin strips
4cm $(1\frac{1}{2}in)$ long
for straps

X←straps→X

B   B

topstitch

B
SATCHEL - SIDE
PANEL Cut 2
leather or felt
A

SUSAN'S HAT

CROWN SECTION

Cut 5   FELT

Ginger

Ginger stands 39cm (15½in) high. She wears her long hair in two plaits and has a smock dress made from a pretty cotton print with a contrasting collar. Ginger's rather pensive I-need-a-cuddle expression makes her everyone's favourite.

Materials and equipment

- Flesh-coloured stockinette
- Iron-on woven interfacing
- Flesh-coloured calico
- Scraps of flesh-coloured or white felt
- Set of 3cm (1¼in) plastic joints
- About 55cm (22in) bright auburn mohair or alpaca roving (for the hair)
- Thin card to make templates of pattern pieces
- White polyester toy filling
- Stuffing sticks
- Fabric paints; permanent markers; colour pencils (see face painting, pages 10–11)
- White tacky craft glue
- Hot-glue gun
- Basic sewing kit, including strong thread and threads to match all fabrics (including those for the clothes)

Clothes

Pants Thin stockinette; narrow elastic; narrow lace trim

Underslip White cotton or polycotton; broderie anglaise trim, 15mm (½in) wide; small button

Dress Cotton print in a small floral design in shades of pink; plain cotton for collar; snap fasteners or decorative buttons

Socks Pair of child's white socks

Pink ribbon 15mm (½in) wide

> Read *Making the Dolls* on pages 8–11
> before you begin.

Ginger wears bought sandals and carries a small handmade or bought teddy bear. Her body is made from stockinette. Before you use stockinette you must stabilize it by fusing woven interfacing to the reverse side. Do not use non-woven interfacing or it will tear when the doll is stuffed, and do not stretch the stockinette when you iron the interfacing to it. Once it is applied, use the fabric as usual.

Making the doll
Follow the instructions for making David up to the hair (see page 60).

The hair
Follow the instructions for Cassie Marie's hair (see pages 32–3) but use the mohair or alpaca roving instead of strands of mohair knitting yarn. The roving must not be combed through. Cut off the amount required and spread it gently with the fingers to cover the tape. Separate the strands with your fingers before plaiting. The wispy curls around the hairline are made by winding thin strands of mohair around a pencil and steaming them with an iron. When they are dry, glue them in place.

Making the clothes
Make the pants, underslip and socks exactly as Amy's (see pages 17 and 19).

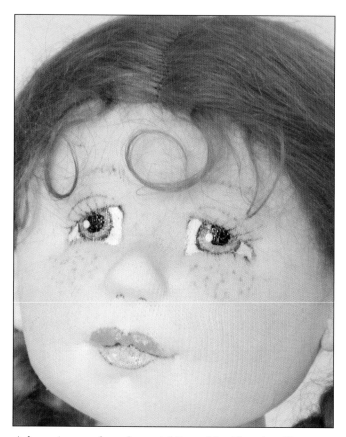

A few wispy curls and a sprinkling of freckles give Ginger a winsome look.

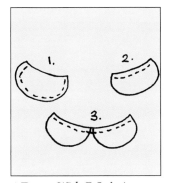

1 Dress. With R.S. facing, sew the collars together in pairs. Clip the curves, turn R.S. out and press. Tack the collars together at the centre front.

2 Sew the collars to the dress bodice, matching the centre fronts.

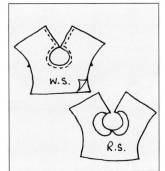

3 With R.S. facing, sew the bodice lining to the bodice at the back openings and around the neckline. Turn R.S. out and press.

4 Gather the top edge of the skirt front between the armholes, pull up gathers to fit the bodice and stitch the skirt front to the bodice.

5 Neaten the facings of the skirt backs and press to the W.S.

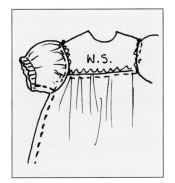

6 Gather the tops of the skirt backs between the armholes and stitch the skirt backs to the bodice backs.

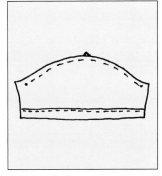

7 Press the hem allowance of sleeves to the W.S. and make casings for narrow elastic. Gather the tops of sleeves between dots.

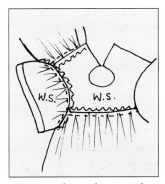

8 Pull up the gathers. With R.S. facing, sew the sleeves into the armholes.

9 Thread narrow elastic through the sleeve casing to fit the doll. Sew side and sleeve seams, securing the elastic in the seams.

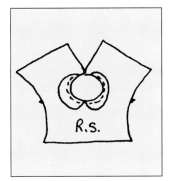

10 Turn the dress R.S. out and press. Press up and sew the hem. Sew snap fasteners or buttons to the back openings.

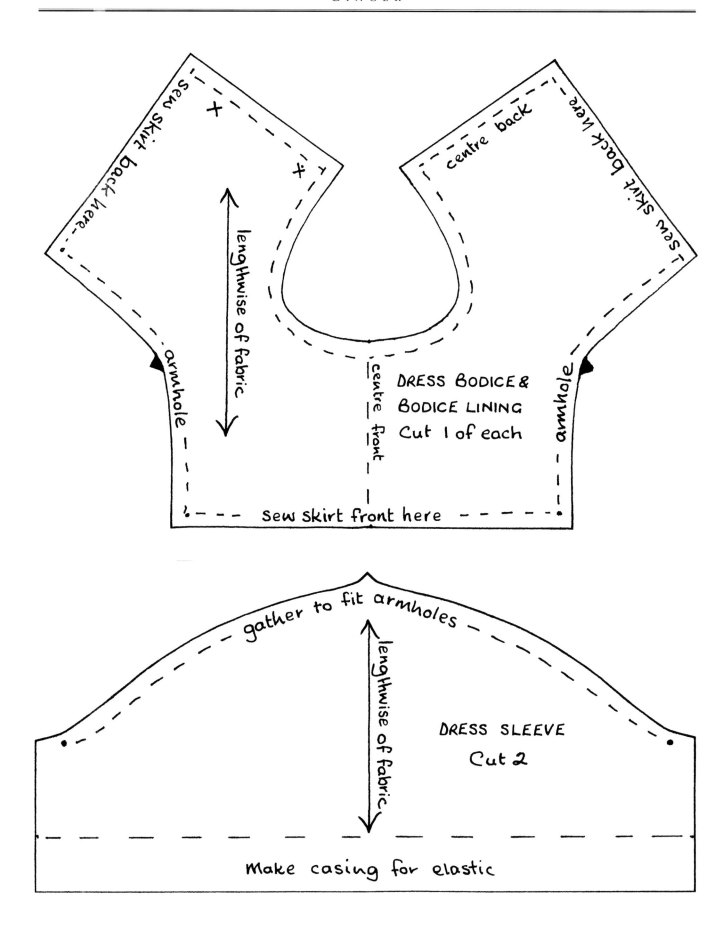

sew skirt back here

X X

centre back

sew skirt back here

lengthwise of fabric

armhole

centre front

armhole

DRESS BODICE &
BODICE LINING
Cut 1 of each

sew skirt front here

gather to fit armholes

lengthwise of fabric

DRESS SLEEVE
Cut 2

Make casing for elastic

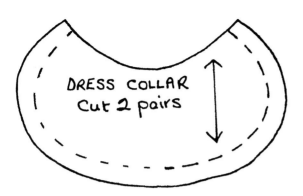

DRESS COLLAR
Cut 2 pairs

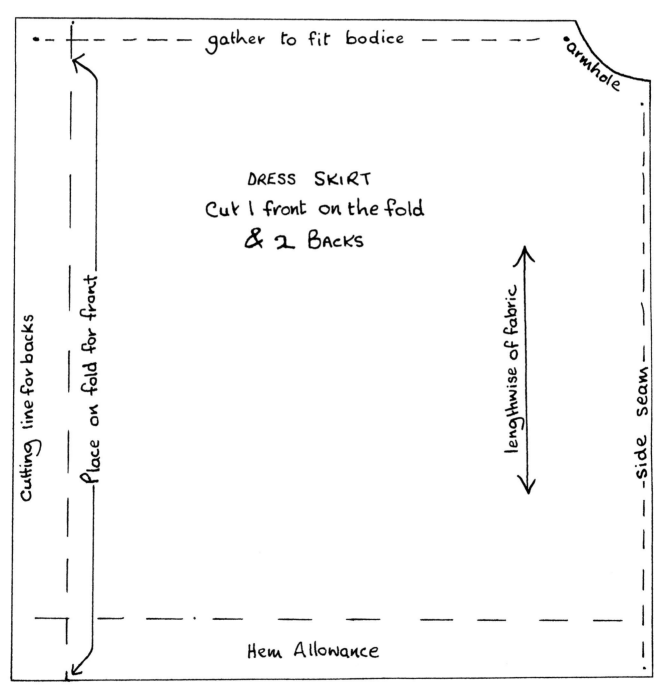

gather to fit bodice

armhole

Cutting line for backs

Place on fold for front

DRESS SKIRT
Cut 1 front on the fold
& 2 Backs

lengthwise of fabric

side seam

Hem Allowance

Pure Needlesculpture

Basically, needle sculpture is simply a method of defining the contours of the face and body by using needle and thread to form ridges and dimples in all the right places. It may seem complicated at first, but with practice it becomes much easier and therefore more enjoyable. There are no hard and fast rules in needle-sculpture – it is an art form.

Once the basics have been learned, most people enjoy experimenting and are fascinated by their creations, often producing wonderful original dolls. Needle-sculpture is not a new technique: it has been used in doll-making for many years. There were many wonderful cloth doll-makers in Britain and America in the early part of the 20th century. I was captivated the first time I saw a picture of Julia Beecher's 'Missionary Ragbabies'. They were made of old silk underwear, skilfully needlesculptured and delicately painted. These beautiful old dolls inspired me to try my hand, and for

The bridge of the nose and the nostrils are formed first.

The nose is completed and the remaining features are sketched in.

The eyes and mouth are needle-sculpted before painting.

Poppy
An example of a completed needle-sculpted and painted face.

years I made baby dolls from nylon stockings and tights – a frustrating process because quite often a ladder or hole would appear just as I was adding the finishing touches, but I gained a lot of experience.

I think there is a limit to what can be learned from a pattern, and this is certainly true of needlesculpture. Use these few easy patterns as a springboard for your own ideas and then practise, practise, practise. If you love making dolls as much as I do you will find that it is worth it in the end.

If you are new to needlesculpture you may find the following points will help you avoid common mistakes.

1 Always check the direction of maximum stretch before tracing patterns.

2 One side of the fabric is a little smoother than the other; choose which one you want as the 'right side' before tracing and cutting.

3 Use a new ballpoint needle in your machine.

4 Strengthen holes made for joints by coating with fray-check.

5 Dolls made for needlesculpture should be stuffed firmly but not too hard: about the feel of a ripe tomato is a good rule of thumb.

Needlesculpture instructions

1 Always begin with an anchor stitch (see below).

2 Try to cut enough thread to finish each sequence. If you think you will run out, exit the needle at a suitable spot and finish off while there is enough thread left. A new thread can be joined anywhere on the face using an anchor stitch.

3 Always exit the thread at a seam or some unobtrusive place and finish off with a small backstitch.

4 After finishing, clip the thread carefully to avoid making a hole in the fabric. If a hole is made accidentally coat it with fray-check and leave to dry. Holes made on the face will always be visible.

5 Dig deep under the stuffing to raise ridges for noses etc. Use the point of a needle to lift the stuffing and move it about under the fabric.

6 Do not pull the stitches too tight.

7 Repeat each stitch at least once to make sure it holds.

8 Use a fine polyester sewing thread in a matching or neutral colour.

9 Stitches shown on the diagrams as dotted lines are underneath the fabric and stuffing.

10 Measurements are approximate and may be adjusted.

How to thread and make an anchor stitch

Cut twice the amount of thread needed. Use a fine darning needle,
about size 2 or 3 for the face, and thread it with both cut ends.

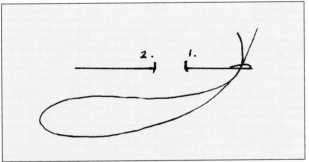

1 Insert the needle at the first point of work. Bring it out at the second point.

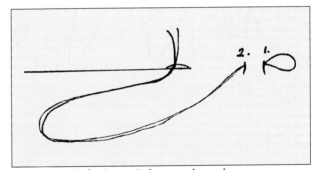

2 Do not pull the loop all the way through.

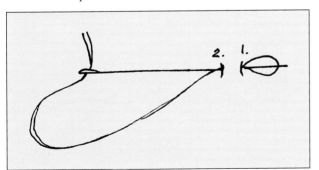

3 Re-insert the needle at almost the same (second) point. Bring it out at the first point, taking the needle point through the loop.

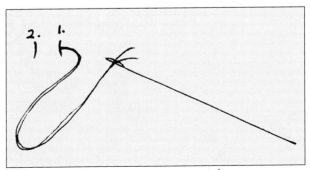

4 Pull the stitch up snugly but not too tight.

Thomas and Friends

Thomas (opposite) is a 36cm (14in) high, cute, cuddly baby boy with jointed arms and legs and a wispy wig, which is easily made from a patch of fur fabric. The terry nappy, one-piece romper and pom-pom slippers he wears would be considered very old fashioned by today's modern babies.

Brown-eyed Bobby is cosy in his fleecy pram coat and bobble hat. Underneath he is wearing a terry nappy and a matinée jacket, and felt booties on his feet.

Rosie, the baby girl above, has a bonnet to match her coat and a pretty, full-skirted smock dress underneath the coat.

Materials and equipment

- Flesh-coloured Windsor Ponte or Comfort
- Set of 3cm (1¼in) plastic joints (for the arms); set of 3.5cm (1½in) plastic joints (for the legs)
- Hair material of your choice – e.g., pack of curly doll hair, small piece of long fur fabric, short length of mohair roving (only loose combings are used)
- Thin card to make templates of pattern pieces
- White polyester toy filling
- Stuffing sticks
- Fabric paints; permanent markers; colour pencils
- Hot-glue gun
- Tacky glue
- 9cm (3½in) doll-making needle
- Basic sewing kit, including strong thread and threads to match all fabrics (including those for the clothes)

Clothes

Nappy Stretch terry cloth; touch-and-close tape

Matinée jacket T-shirt fabric or other soft fabric; embroidery thread; narrow ribbon

Dress and rompers Any soft fabrics, either plain or with small patterns or dots; narrow elastic; small buttons or snap fasteners

Coats and hats Acrylic fleece in soft colours; matching buttons; ribbon 7mm (about ¼in) wide; 1 pompon

Socks Pair of baby white socks (for each doll)

Booties and slippers Felt; narrow ribbon; small buttons; small pompons

Read *Making the Dolls* on pages 8–11 before you begin.

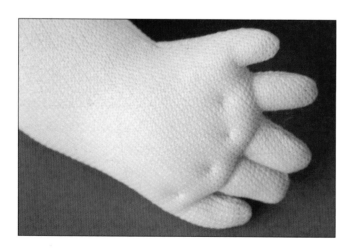

Windsor Ponte
The material used for the body must be a firm knit with a little stretch. Windsor Ponte, a knit fabric that is very strong and does not run when stretched, is ideal, but you can use other fabrics if you prefer. Windsor Comfort is lighter in weight and smoother to the touch. Knitted velour is also suitable, and you can use either the smooth or the fuzzy side.

Styling Thomas and Friends' hair

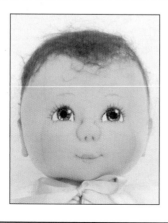

Bobby's sparse baby hair can be made by gluing combings from mohair roving to the doll's head. Use tacky craft glue, which dries clear.

Rosie's curly hair is made from a purchased pack of curly craft hair. The curls are glued to her head using a hot-glue gun.

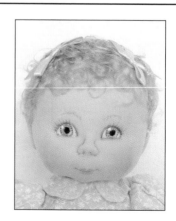

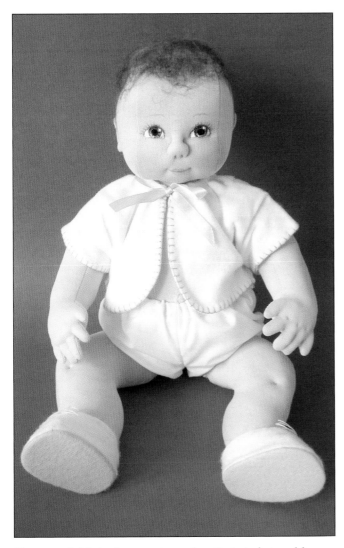

Choose soft fabrics for nappies and matinée jackets, add a little simple stitching and tie with a satin ribbon.

Rosie is wearing a traditional smock dress with a full skirt. It is in a pretty pastel pink to tone with her coat and bonnet.

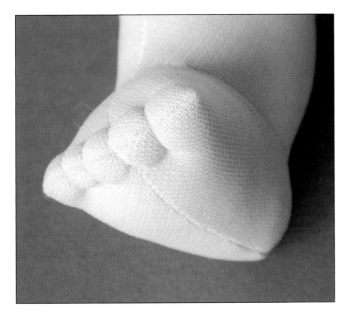

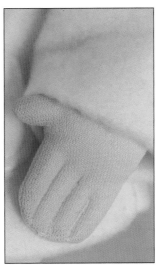

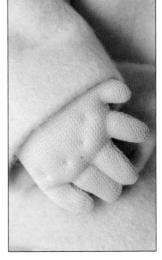

Stitch little toes and fingers on the baby dolls. Define fingers by top-stitching or use the pattern with separate fingers.

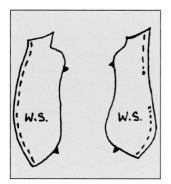

1 Body. Sew the centre-front seam of the body front. Sew the centre-back seam of the body back, leaving it open between the dots.

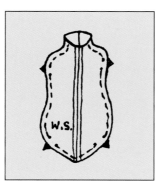

2 With R.S. facing, sew body front to body back, leaving small openings for the joint pegs. Turn R.S. out. Tack the neck seam allowance to the inside.

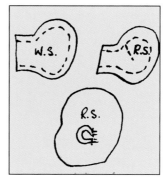

3 Ears. Sew the ears, turn R.S. out, stuff lightly and top-stitch. Sew the ears to the R.S. of the head so that they are facing forward.

4 Head. Sew the chin dart in head centre. With R.S. facing, sew head sides to head centre. Turn R.S. out and stay-stitch the neck edge.

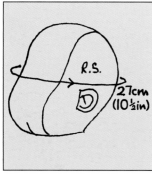

5 Stuff the head. The stuffed head should measure about 27cm (10½in) all round. Fold back the ears and stitch in place.

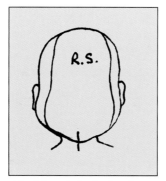

6 Ladder-stitch the head to the body so that it either faces straight forward or turns to one side, which looks more natural when the doll is lying down.

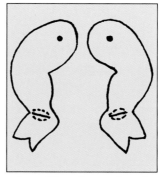

7 Legs. Place the insides of the legs side by side to make sure you have a right and a left. Clip or punch small holes for the joint pegs.

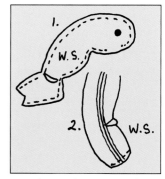

8 With R.S. facing, sew the legs, leaving open between dots. Pinch up and sew the darts on the insides of the ankles. Flatten out the feet and sew across the toes.

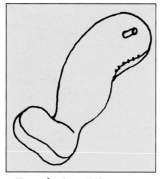

9 Turn the legs R.S. out. Stuff the legs and insert the joints. Ladder-stitch the openings.

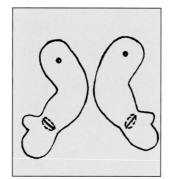

10 Arms. Lay the insides of the arms side by side. Clip or punch small holes for the joints.

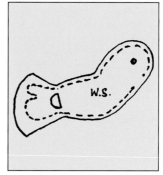

11 With R.S. facing, sew the arms. The hands are templates. If you are using the separate fingers, see page 54. Sew the wrist darts.

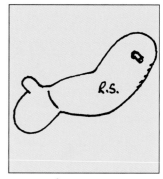

12 Turn the arms R.S. out. Stuff the arms and insert the joints. Ladder-stitch the openings.

Do not join the arms and legs to the body until after the needle-modelling of the head is completed.

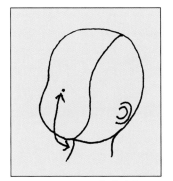

13 Measure 6cm (2½in) from the neck to the centre of the head centre panel. Mark this point with a straight pin.

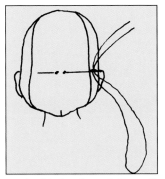

14 At this level mark 2 small dots, 1cm (½in) apart. This is the bridge of the nose and the starting point for needle-modelling. Make an anchor stitch at this point.

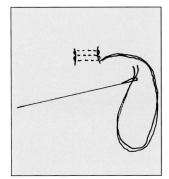

15 Continue to work a few rows back and forth underneath the stuffing to form the bridge of the nose.

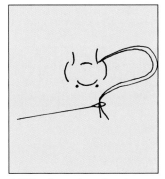

16 Use the point of a strong needle to pull up a small bump in the stuffing to form the nose. Mark the nostrils about 1cm (½in) apart under the nose.

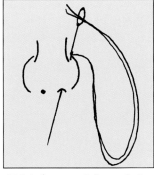

17 Stitch up and down 2–3 times from the bridge to the nostril, digging under the stuffing. Do not pull too tight. Bring the thread out at the bridge of the nose.

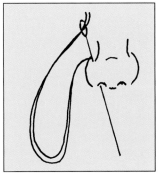

18 Take the needle under the bridge to the other side. Work the second nostril. Bring the thread out at the bridge of the nose.

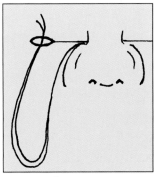

19 Use a sharp pencil to draw a curved line either side of the nose, from the bridge to just below the nostrils. This will define the shape of the nose but will be wider than the finished nose.

20 Start at bridge and work down in a ladder formation. Use the curved lines as a guide. Dig under the stuffing to lift the nose. The pencil lines should be covered in small, neat stitches. Exit thread at the bottom.

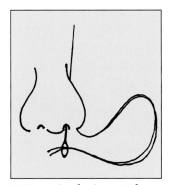

21 To make the last stitch, insert the needle just below the nostril and bring it out at the bridge. Repeat at the other side. At this point you may want to re-define the nostrils.

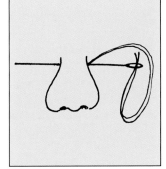

22 To finish off, stitch back and forth across the bridge a few times. Bring out the needle at the neck seam and clip the thread carefully.

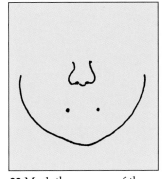

23 Mark the corners of the mouth slightly lower than you plan the mouth to be, about 15mm (⅝in) below the nose and 15mm (⅝in) apart.

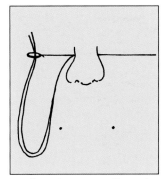

24 Thread your needle and make an anchor stitch just below the bridge of the nose.

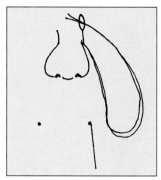

25 Stitch from nose to mouth corner and pull up the thread slightly but not too tight. Repeat once or twice to hold the stitch.

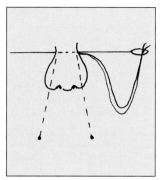

26 Cross the bridge and repeat at the other side, keeping both sides even. Bring out the needle at the neck seam and clip the thread carefully.

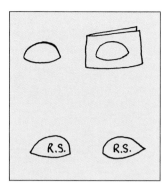

27 Make a card template of the eye shape. Fold a piece of paper in half, trace the eye onto it and cut it out. You now have a pair of eye templates. Mark the R.S. to avoid confusion.

28 Pin the templates to the face so that they are about level with the top of the nose and about an eye's width apart. Draw around them with a sharp pencil.

29 Thread a long needle. Starting at the neck seam make an anchor stitch (see page 77). Stitch from the neck to the outer corner of one eye, pull up slightly and stitch back and forth to hold the stitch. Repeat at the inner corner of the eye. Bring the needle out at the neck and clip the thread. Rethread the needle and repeat at the other eye. See face painting (pages 10–11) to finish the face. Draw the mouth line lightly with a tan marker pen. Thomas could have a simple line mouth or a more detailed one with rosy lips coloured with a warm pink crayon pencil.

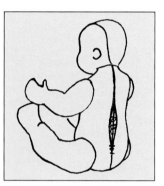

30 Join the legs and arms to the body. Stuff the body and ladder-stitch the openings.

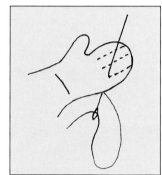

31 Top-stitch to define the fingers.

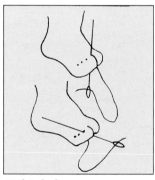

32 Stitch the toes.

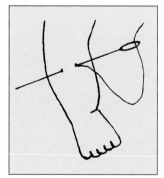

33 Stitch back and forth a few times to make dimples in the knees and elbows.

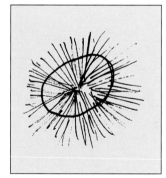

34 Cut out the wispy wig from long fur fabric and brush out.

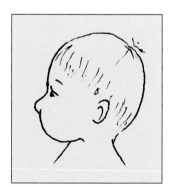

35 Pin, then stitch the wig in place on the crown of the head. Smear the head all around the wig with tacky glue, brush the fur over and leave to dry.

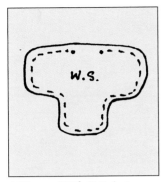

1 Nappy. With R.S. facing, sew the lining to the nappy, leaving an opening between the dots.

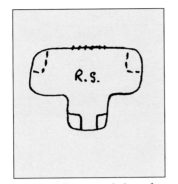

2 Turn R.S. out and close the opening. Sew the touch-and-close tape in place.

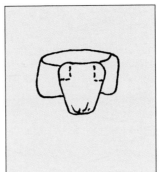

3 To fasten, wrap the side flaps around the doll and the front flap over them.

4 Matinée jacket. With R.S. facing, sew the lining to the jacket along the front edges and neck, back hem and sleeve hems. Leave small openings at the neck edge for ribbon.

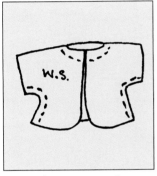

5 Clip the corners and curves and turn R.S. out. Sew the underarm seams. Top-stitch the neck edge to make a casing for ribbon.

6 Turn R.S. out. Top-stitch or blanket-stitch the edge for decoration. Thread ribbon through the casing.

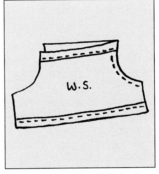

7 Knickers. With R.S. facing, sew the centre-front seam. Make casings at the waist edge and hems of both legs.

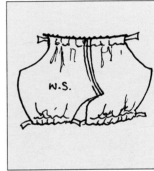

8 Thread the waist and leg casings with elastic to fit the doll.

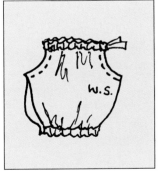

9 Sew the centre-back seam, securing elastic in the seam.

10 Sew the crotch seam, also securing the elastic. Turn R.S. out.

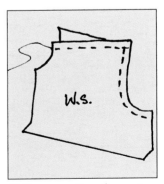

11 Dress. See Ginger's dress (page 73).

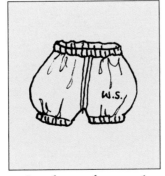

12 Rompers. Sew the centre-front seam of the romper front. Open out and gather the top edge between the armholes.

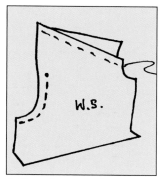

13 Sew the centre-back seam to the dot. Gather top edges between the armholes.

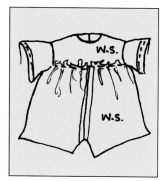

14 Make the romper bodice and collar the same way as the dress. Sew the romper front, backs and sleeves to the bodice.

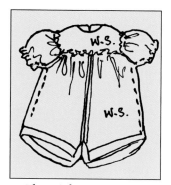

15 Thread the sleeve casings with elastic to fit the doll. Sew the side seams. Make casings at the leg edges.

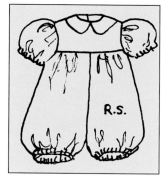

16 Thread elastic through the leg casings to fit the doll and sew the crotch seam. Turn romper R.S. out. Sew on snap fasteners.

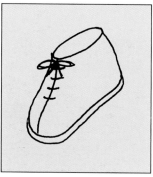

17 Booties. Follow the directions for Andrew's shoes (page 19). Make the socks as Andrew's (page 19).

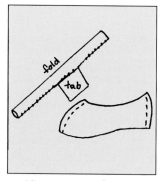

18 Slippers. Fold the strap in half and oversew the edges together. Sew the centre-front and centre-back seams.

19 Gather the lower edges and pull up gathers sufficiently to hold the cardboard sole in place. Cover the second card sole.

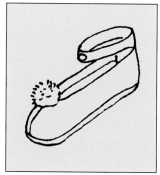

20 Ladder-stitch the sole to shoe. Sew the tab inside the back of the shoe. Try the shoe on the doll and sew on a snap fastener and button. Stick or sew a pompon to the front.

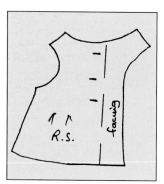

21 Coat. Mark the buttonholes and pocket placements with thread on the R.S. Press the fold line for the facing to the W.S.

22 With R.S. facing, sew the shoulder seams.

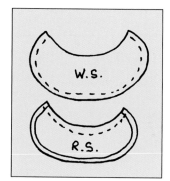

23 Sew around the collar, turn R.S. out, press and tack the raw edges together. Top-stitch the finished edge.

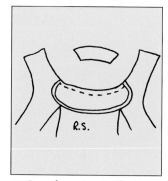

24 Sew the collar to the R.S. of the neckline, matching the centre of collar to the centre back of the coat.

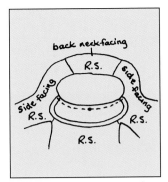

25 With R.S. facing, sew the back neck facing to the side facings.

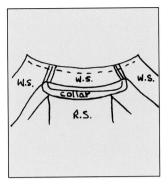

26 Sew the facings in place over the collar through all thicknesses.

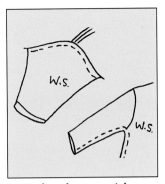

27 Gather the tops of the sleeves between dots to ease. Sew sleeves in place. Sew sleeve and side seams.

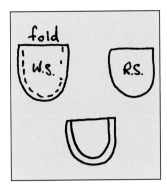

28 Fold pockets in half, R.S. facing, and stitch, leaving openings to turn. Turn R.S. out. Top-stitch pockets onto the coat.

29 Hem the coat and sleeves. Top-stitch the front openings. Make buttonholes and sew on buttons.

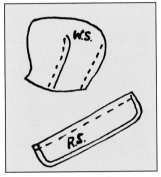

30 Bonnet. Sew both back seams of the bonnet. Make the brim in the same way as the coat collar.

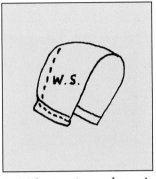

31 Make a casing at the neck edge of the bonnet.

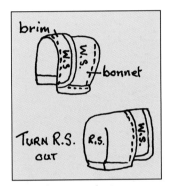

32 With R.S. of the brim facing W.S. of the bonnet, sew the brim in place, leaving the casings free.

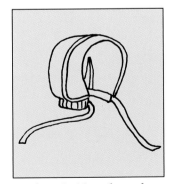

33 Thread ribbon through the casing and pull it up to fit the doll's neck. Sew the ribbon in place and neaten the openings of the casing.

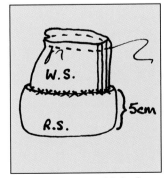

34 Bobble hat. Fold the hat with R.S. facing and sew the centre-back seam. Turn a 5cm (2in) hem to the W.S. Sew with stretch-stitch or hem loosely.

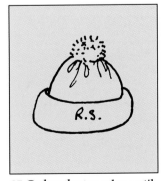

35 Gather the top edge until it is tightly closed and finish off securely. Turn R.S. out. Turn the brim to the R.S. and sew a pompon to the top.

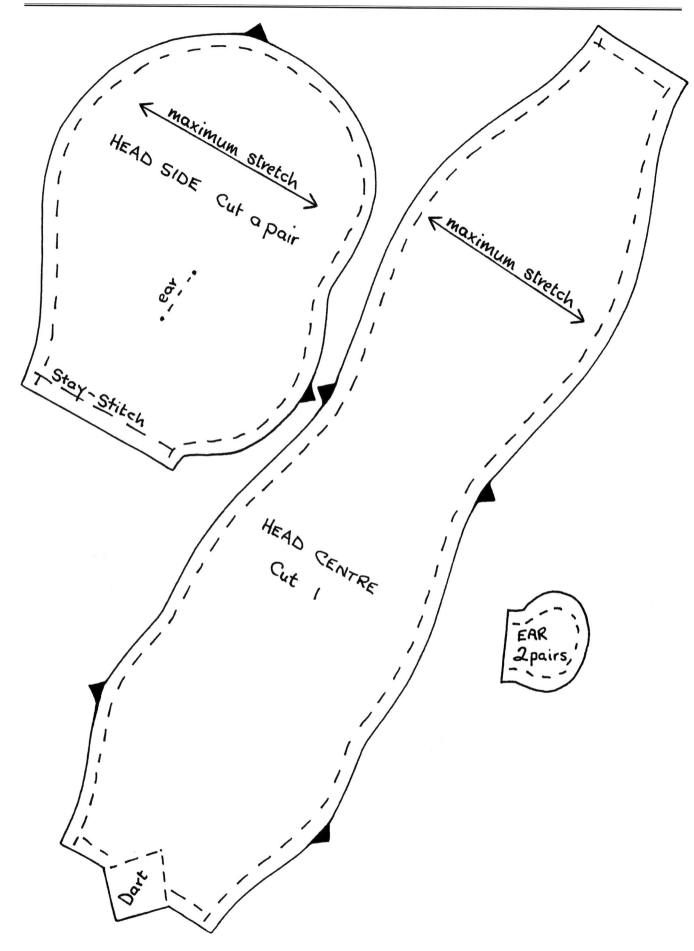

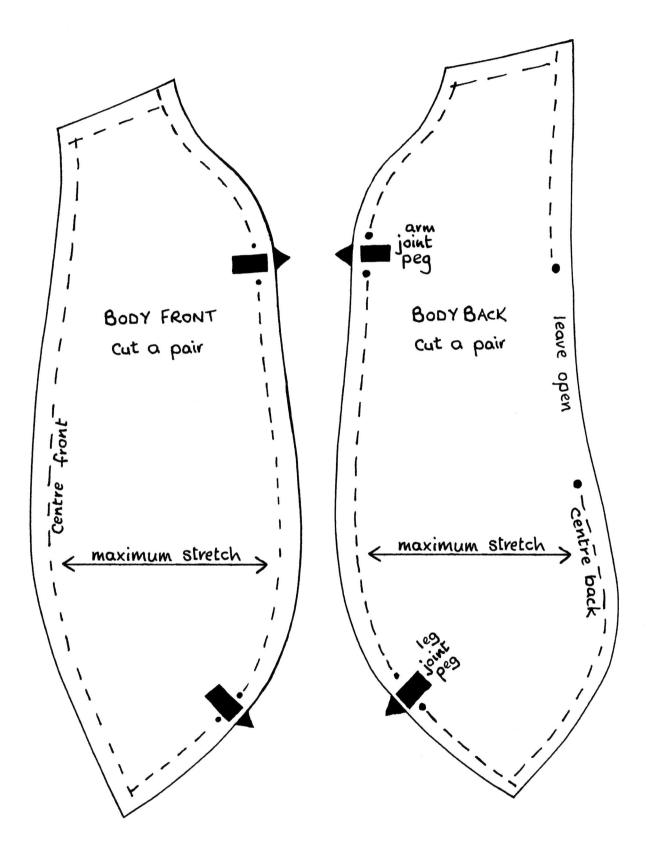

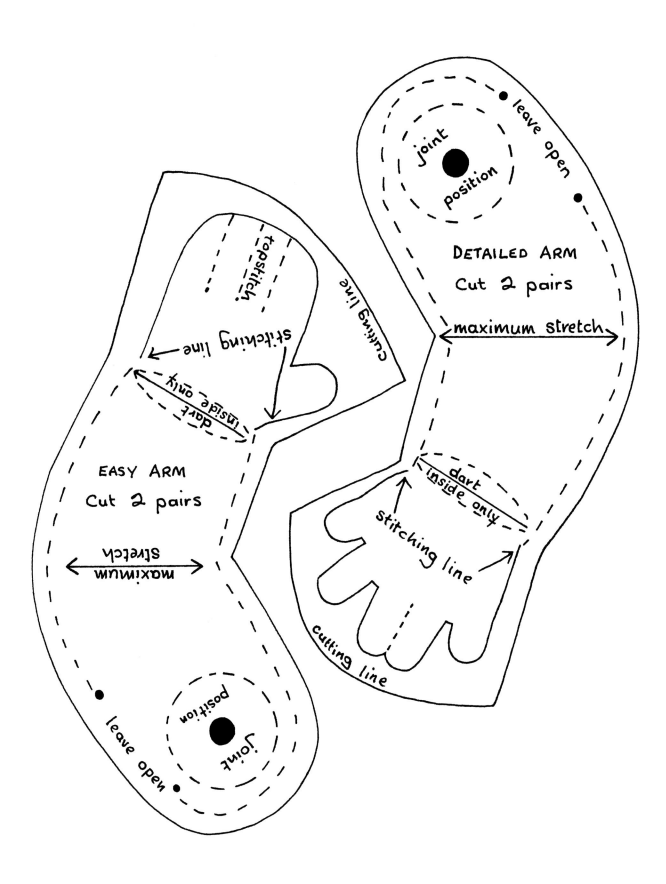

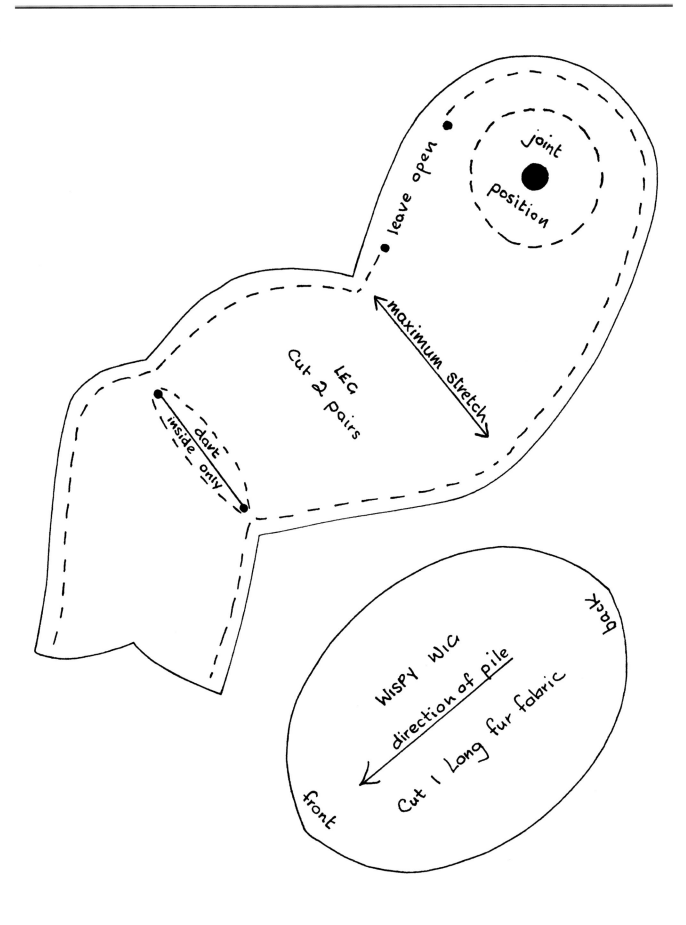

Joint position

leave open

maximum stretch

LEG
Cut 2 Pairs

dart
inside only

WISPY WIG
direction of pile
Cut 1 Long fur fabric

back

front

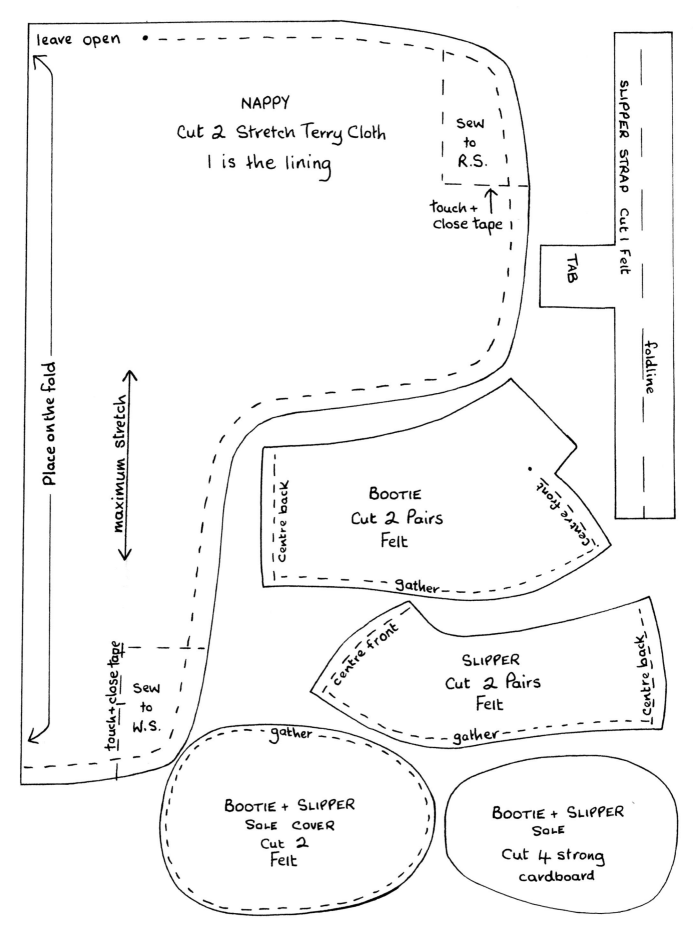

leave open

NAPPY
Cut 2 Stretch Terry Cloth
1 is the lining

Sew to R.S.

touch + Close tape

SLIPPER STRAP Cut 1 Felt

TAB

foldline

Place on the fold

maximum stretch

Centre back

BOOTIE
Cut 2 Pairs
Felt

centre front

gather

touch + close tape

Sew to W.S.

Centre front

SLIPPER
Cut 2 Pairs
Felt

centre back

gather

gather

gather

BOOTIE + SLIPPER
Sole Cover
Cut 2
Felt

BOOTIE + SLIPPER
Sole
Cut 4 strong
cardboard

92

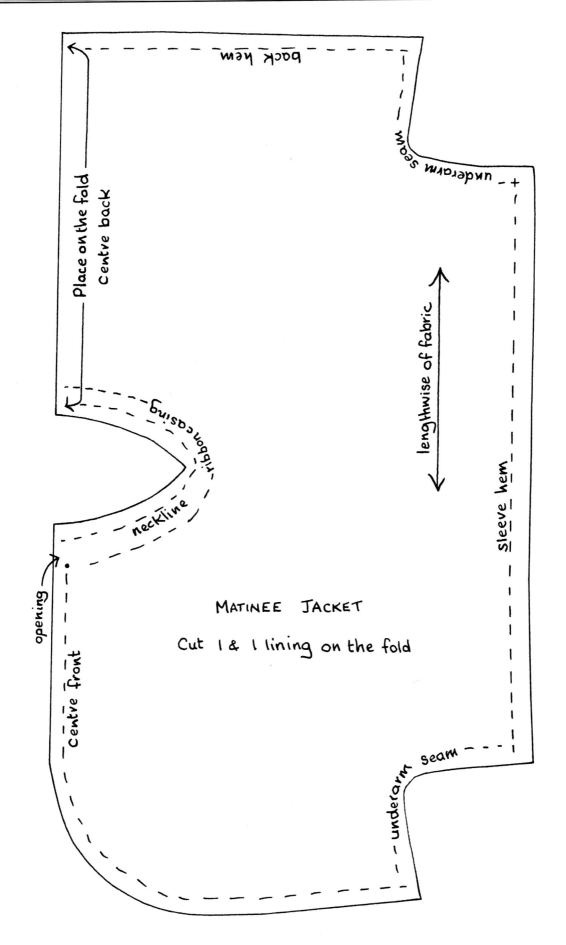

MATINEE JACKET

Cut 1 & 1 lining on the fold

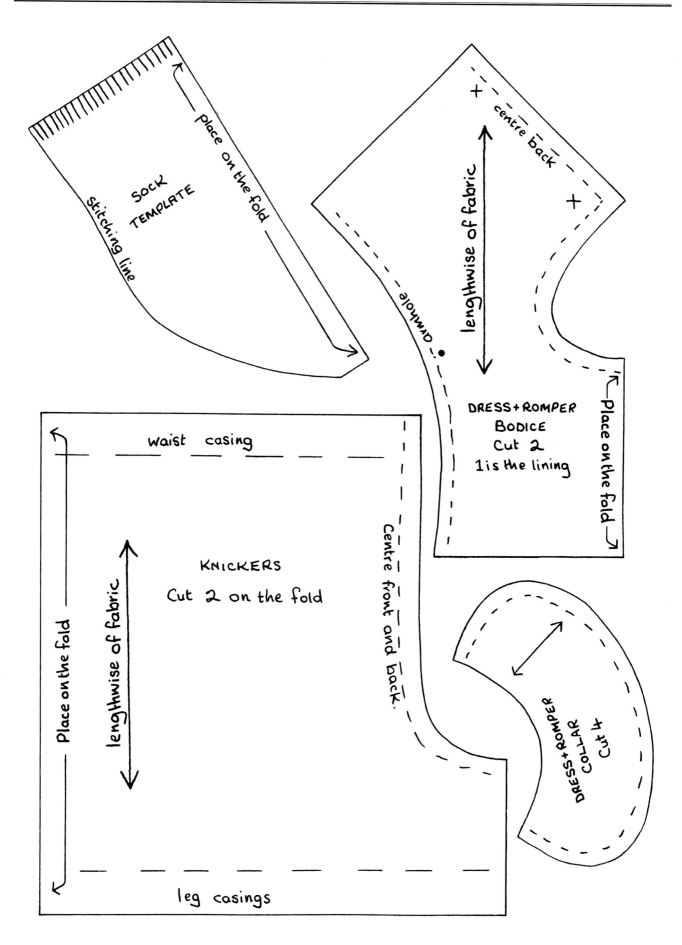

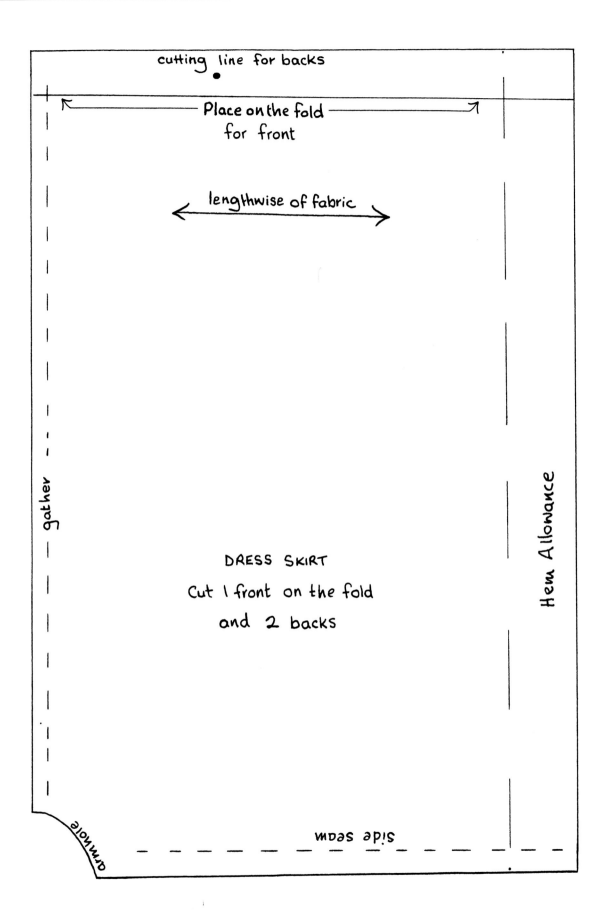

cutting line for backs

Place on the fold
for front

lengthwise of fabric

gather

Hem Allowance

DRESS SKIRT

Cut 1 front on the fold

and 2 backs

armhole

Side seam

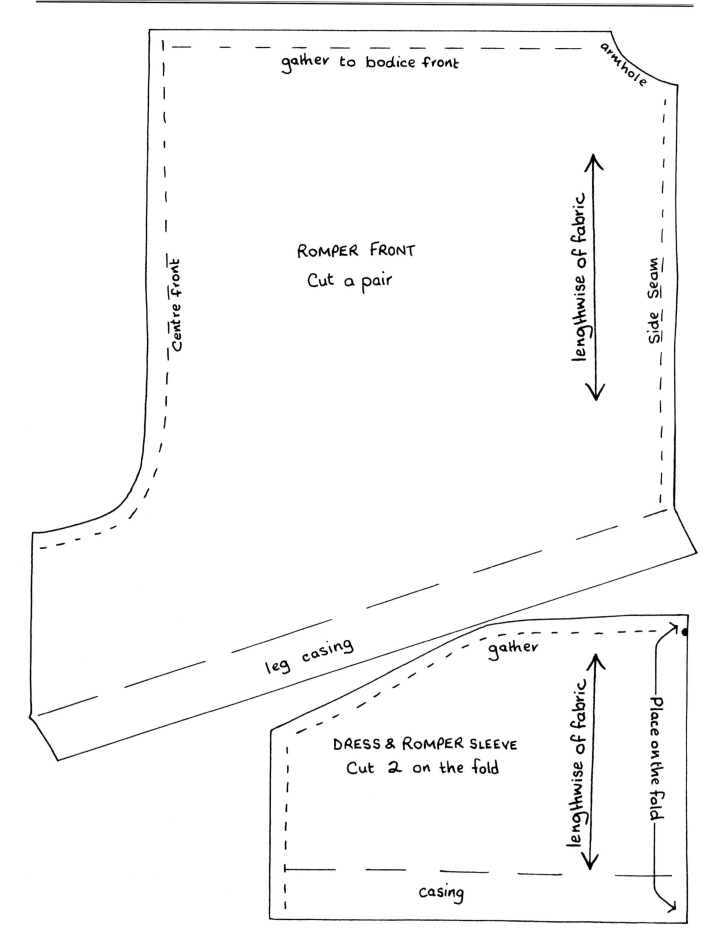

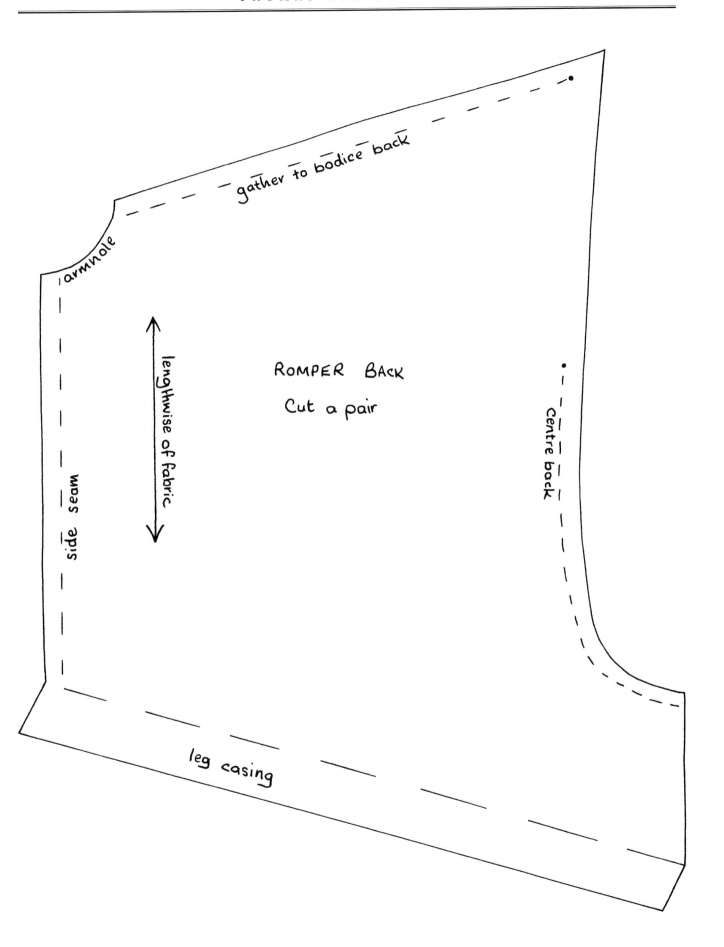

gather to bodice back

armhole

lengthwise of fabric

ROMPER BACK

Cut a pair

side seam

Centre back

leg casing

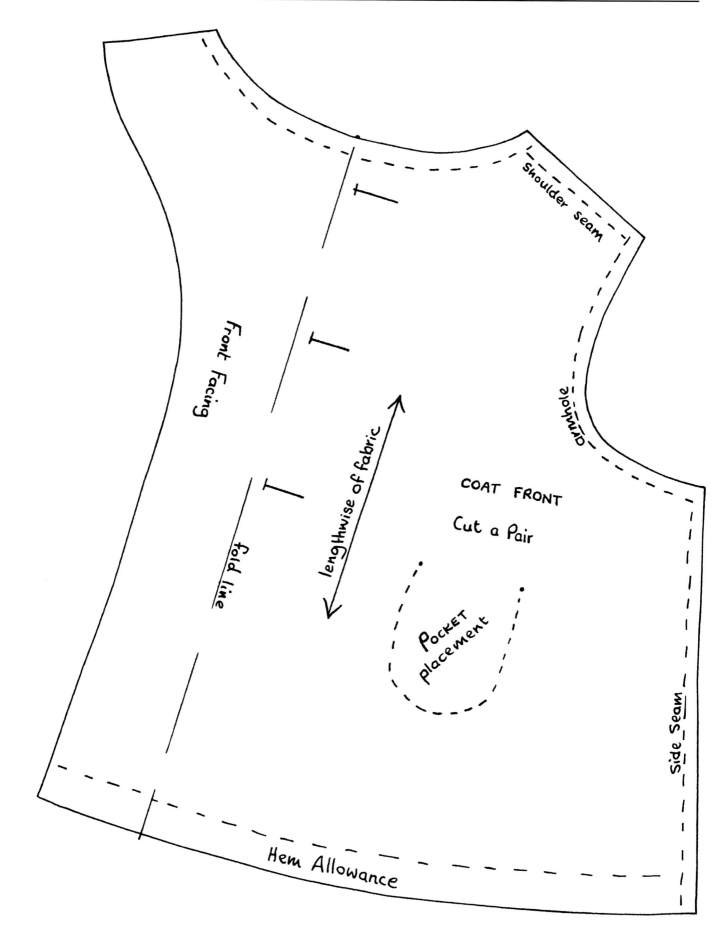

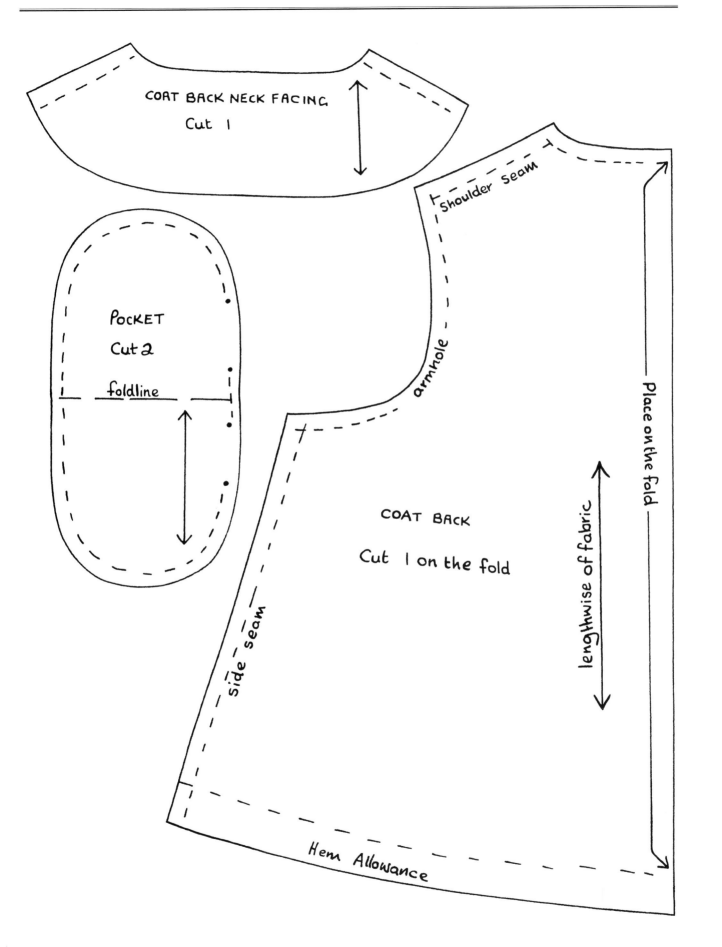

COAT BACK NECK FACING

Cut 1

POCKET

Cut 2

foldline

Shoulder seam

armhole

COAT BACK

Cut 1 on the fold

lengthwise of fabric

Place on the fold

side seam

Hem Allowance

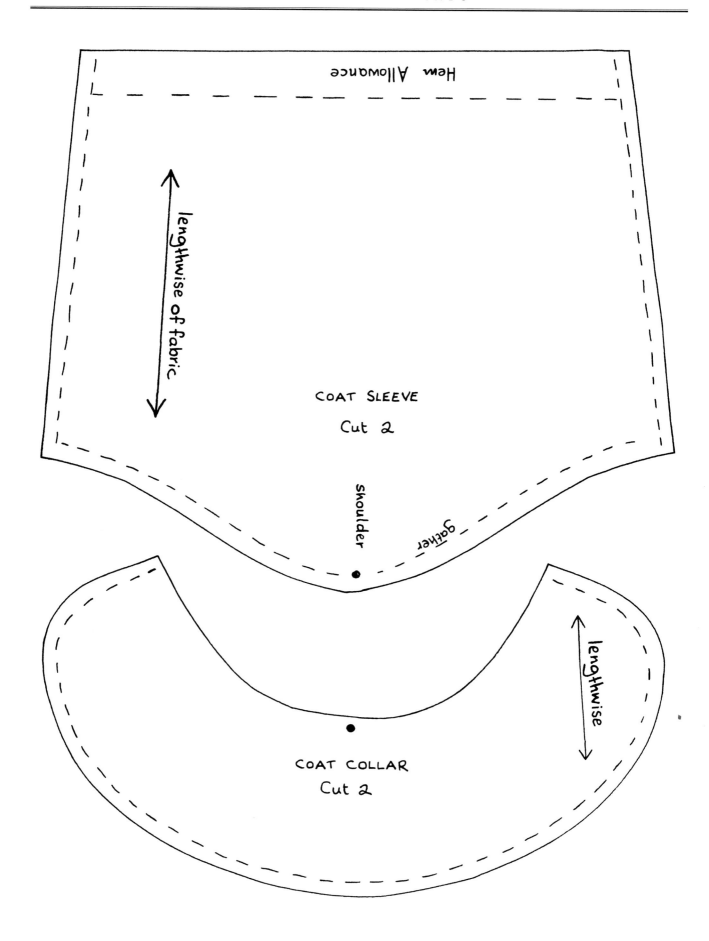

COAT SLEEVE

Cut 2

COAT COLLAR

Cut 2

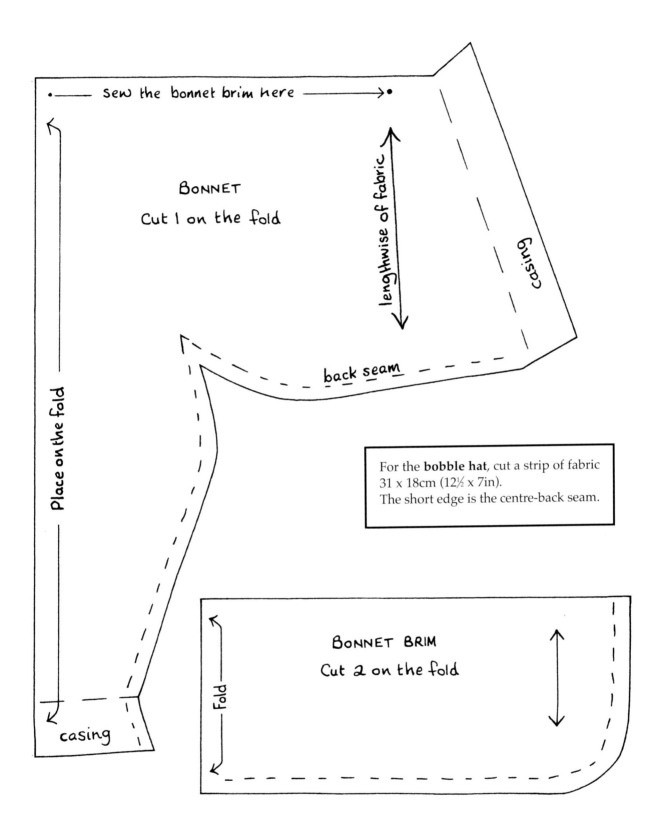

sew the bonnet brim here

BONNET

Cut 1 on the fold

lengthwise of fabric

casing

back seam

Place on the fold

casing

For the **bobble hat**, cut a strip of fabric 31 x 18cm (12½ x 7in).
The short edge is the centre-back seam.

Fold

BONNET BRIM

Cut 2 on the fold

Poppy

This boudoir doll is 56cm (22in) tall. Poppy is a doll with attitude and is reminiscent of the slender, elegant lady dolls of the 1920s, which were often found decorating the homes and limousines of the fashionable ladies of the time. She has bobbed hair and wears a cloche hat, bar-strap shoes and a long string of beads, which were so popular. Poppy will sit or lounge almost anywhere, but looks particularly comfortable in a small chair of her own.

Materials and equipment

- Unbleached or pale pink calico
- Flesh-coloured Windsor Comfort
- 24 x 12cm (10 x 5in) long fur fabric, black
- 2 small buttons to match the body fabric
- White polyester toy filling
- Stuffing sticks
- Thin card to make templates of pattern pieces
- Black, white, blue and red fabric paints; black and tan permanent markers; blue crayon pencil; peach-coloured cosmetic blusher
- 9cm (3½in) doll-making needle
- Gloss varnish
- Basic sewing kit, including strong thread and threads to match all fabrics (including those for the clothes)

Clothes

Dress Soft cotton or silky fabric, red and white print; 3 small snap fasteners

Knickers Thin white fabric; narrow lace trim; narrow elastic

Hat 30 x 30cm (12 x 12in) red felt

Necklace of small red or black beads 38cm (15in) long

Read *Making the Dolls* on pages 8–11 before you begin.

Poppy is made from two fabrics. The body and legs are made from calico so that she can sit well and to give shape to the shoes. The head, arms and neck cover are needlesculptured fabric. The legs and arms of this pattern are templates.

Sew around the shoes with a very small stitch and clip the curve under the heel up to the stitching. After sewing and trimming the toes, carefully turn them right side out. Stuff the shoes a little at a time very firmly, shaping them as you work.

Poppy's head should measure 21cm (8¼in) all around when stuffed. Stretch the head gently as you work and fill every hollow smoothly, taking care that you do not leave any gaps between the filling.

Poppy's face colours
- eyebrows – black
- eyelid crease – tan
- eyelid – blue crayon pencil
- eyeline and lashes – black
- iris – blue
- pupil – black
- lips and nails – red
- cheeks – peach blusher
- highlights – white

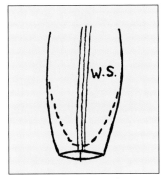

1 Legs and shoes. After sewing and cutting out, flatten out the foot. Trace around the card toe guide and sew the pointed toe.

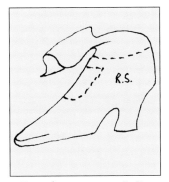

2 Trim the corners and clip curves. Turn R.S. out, taking extra care with the heels and toes. Mark the guidelines for painting the shoes.

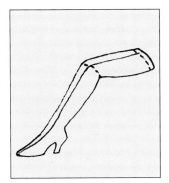

3 Stuff the shoes and legs up to the knees, flattening them out so that the seams are in the centre. Top-stitch across the knees. Stuff the tops of the legs softly. Tack the tops of the legs closed.

4 Paint and varnish the shoes now, while the legs are separate. Lay them aside to dry.

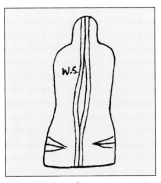

5 Body. Sew the centre-back seam of the body back, leaving an opening. Sew the hip darts.

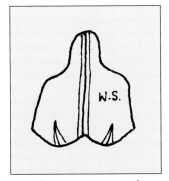

6 With R.S. facing, sew the centre-front seam of the chest and sew the bust darts. Stay-stitch and clip the lower edge of chest and top edge of abdomen.

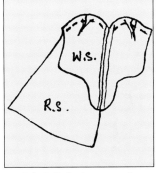

7 With R.S. facing, sew the chest to the abdomen.

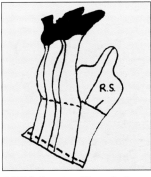

8 With fronts of legs facing the R.S. of the body front, sew the legs in place. Make sure the seam allowance is left free at both sides.

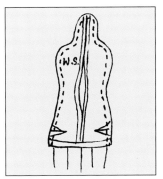

9 Allow the legs to fall forward. With R.S. facing, sew the body back to the body front. Turn R.S. out.

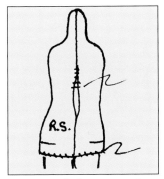

10 Slipstitch the lower edge of the body back to the tops of the legs. Stuff the body firmly, especially the neck and bust. Ladder-stitch the opening.

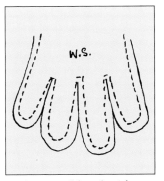

11 Arms and hands. After cutting out the arms, clip carefully between each finger up to the stitching. (See page 54 for turning and stuffing fingers.)

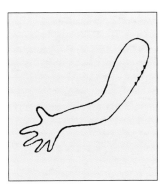

12 Turn arms R.S. out and stuff carefully. Ladder-stitch the openings. Paint on miniature red fingernails later when you paint Poppy's lips.

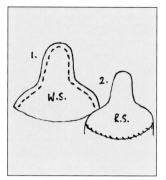

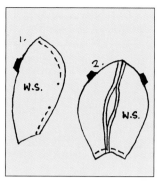

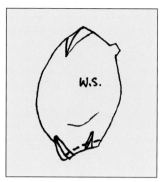

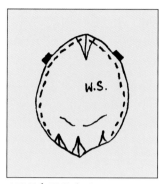

13 Neck cover. With R.S. facing, sew the seam and turn R.S. out. Pull the cover snugly over the neck, turn in the raw edge and stitch neatly to the body.

14 The head. With R.S. facing, sew the centre-back seam of the head back, leaving an opening. Stay-stitch the neck edge.

15 Sew the forehead dart and the 3 chin darts in the head front. Stay-stitch the neck edge.

16 With R.S. facing, sew head front to head back, matching the notches. Turn R.S. out and stuff carefully, shaping the head with your hands as you work.

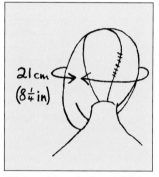

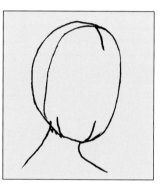

17 Attaching the head. Make a hole in the stuffing with your fingers and push the neck firmly into the head.

18 When you are satisfied with the head position, ladder-stitch it in place.

Attaching the arms

Poppy's arms are button-jointed. The buttons are on the outsides of the arms to strengthen the points where the thread enters the fabric. Thread a long doll-making needle with a long length of doubled strong thread. Follow the sequence shown in the diagram above. Make sure the thumbs face forward before you begin. Keep a tight tension on the thread and pass the needle back and forth several times before finishing off.

Poppy's face

The smaller the face, the more difficult it is to keep the features in proportion. Poppy's head does not use a vast amount of fabric, so I usually make two or three, just in case I am unhappy with my first attempt – and if I end up with three perfect heads, it's a bonus. The nose is worked in exactly the same way as Thomas's; refer to steps 14–22 on page 83 but ignore the measurements. Poppy has a small, delicate nose. Take care that you do not make it too big, and it will be a guide for the rest of her face.

Remember that the measurements are approximate and may be altered slightly. Draw the features lightly in pencil. Use a fine cotton darning needle to model the nose, and a doll-making needle, about 9cm (3½in) long, to indent the eyes and mouth corners. Begin with an anchor stitch.

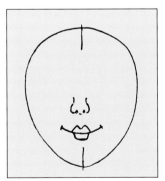

1 Measure 5cm (2in) from the neck to the centre of the face. Mark this point with a pin.

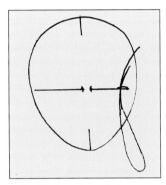

2 At this level mark two small dots 7mm (⅜in) apart. This is the bridge of the nose and the starting point for needle modelling Follow steps 14–17 for Thomas (page 83).

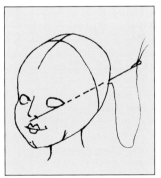

3 For the nostrils and guidelines for the nose see steps 17-19 for Thomas. Follow steps 20–22 to finish the nose.

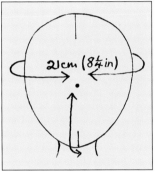

4 Mark with pins 3 points 1cm (½in) below the nose and 2.5cm (1in) apart. Use these as a guide to draw the curved line for Poppy's mouth (the diagram is actual size).

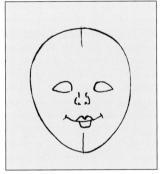

5 Draw the 'bee stung' lips in the centre of the line.

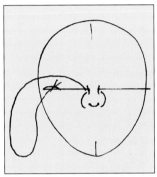

6 Draw the eyes using the templates on page 109. The eyelids are added later.

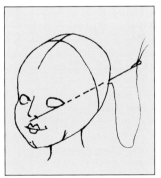

7 Working from the back of the head and using the long needle and strong thread, indent the eye corners. See covered needlesculpture, step 7 (page 56).

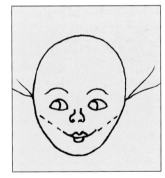

8 Indent the corners of Poppy's mouth from the sides of the head beyond the hairline. Pull on the threads slightly to make her smile.

Making the clothes
To make the knickers and hat, follow the instructions for Cassie Marie's clothes (see pages 33 and 35). The finished hat is very close fitting and should be pulled well down. The crown may need a little stuffing to give it shape.

1 Dress. With R.S. facing, sew the shoulder seams.

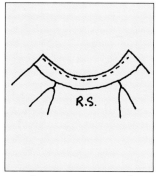

2 With R.S. facing, sew the neckline facing. Clip curves and press to W.S.

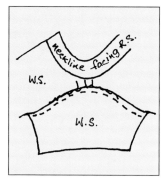

3 Gather the tops of the sleeves between dots. Sew in place.

4 Sew sleeve and side seams.

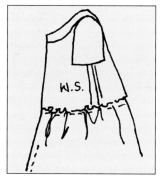

5 Gather one long edge of the dress skirt to fit bodice. Sew in place. Sew the centre-back seam of the skirt for 12cm (5in).

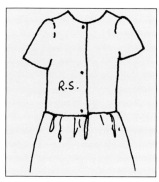

6 Hem the dress and sleeves. Sew snap fasteners to the back opening.

Fur fabric wig

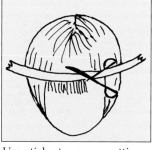

Use sticky tape as a cutting guide.

Re-read the guidelines on page 8 before you cut fur fabric. Face edge and nape are marked on the pattern pieces. Sew the darts at the crown of each piece. With R.S. facing, sew the wig front to the wig back. Turn R.S. out. Brush well to release any fur trapped in the seam. Place the wig on the doll and when you are satisfied with the position, sew it in place. Brush the wig straight down with a fringe. Using small sharp scissors trim to a 1920s 'bob'.

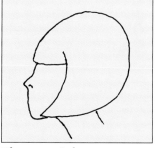

The general shape.

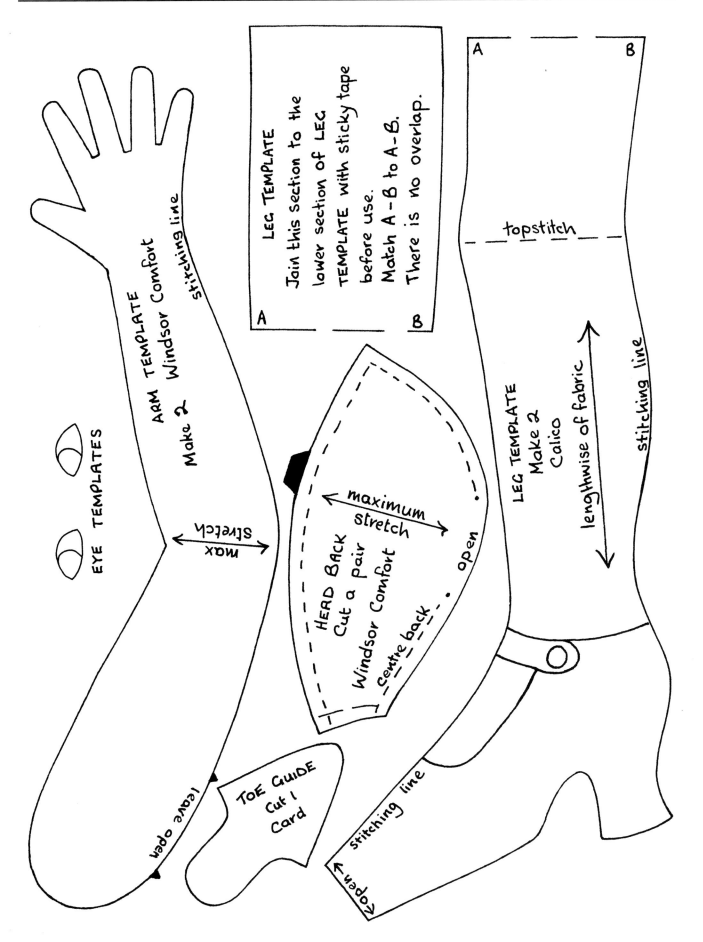

EYE TEMPLATES

ARM TEMPLATE
Windsor Comfort
Make 2

stitching line

max stretch

leave open

LEG TEMPLATE
Join this section to the
lower section of LEG
TEMPLATE with sticky tape
before use.
Match A–B to A–B.
There is no overlap.

A

B

HEAD BACK
Cut a Pair
Windsor Comfort

maximum stretch

open

centre back

TOE GUIDE
Cut 1
Card

stitching line

open

A

B

topstitch

LEG TEMPLATE
Make 2
Calico

lengthwise of fabric

stitching line

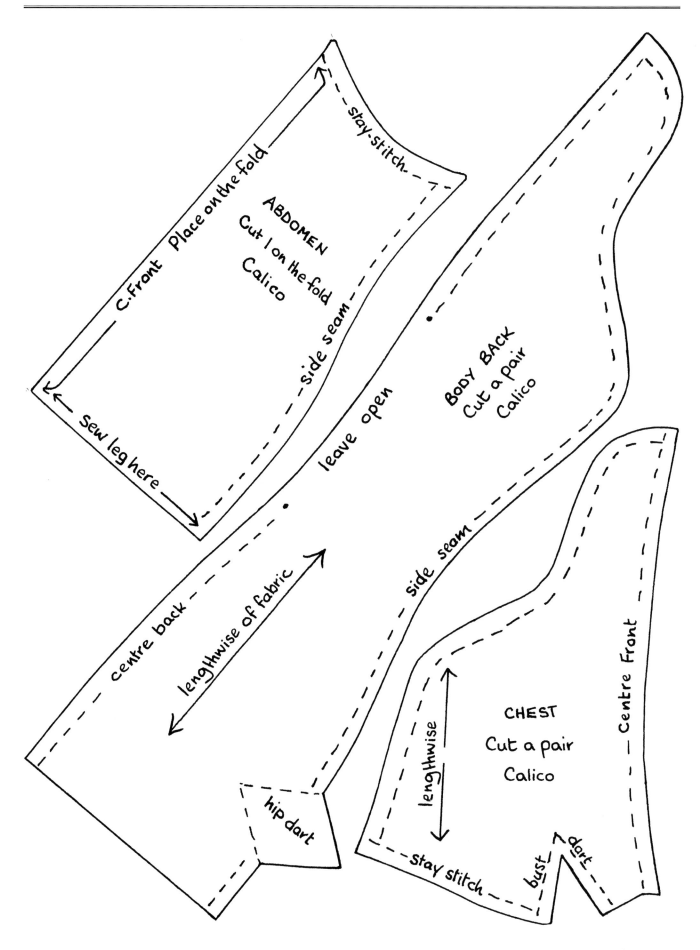

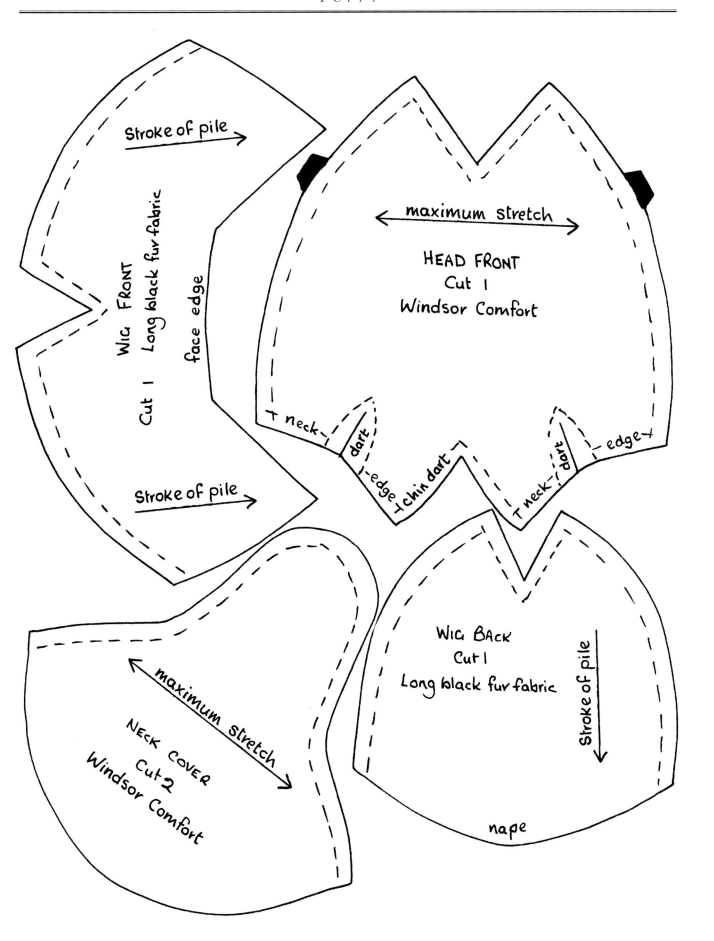

Stroke of pile →

WIG FRONT
Cut 1
Long black fur fabric

face edge

Stroke of pile →

← maximum stretch →

HEAD FRONT
Cut 1
Windsor Comfort

⊤ neck
dart
⊤ edge ⊤ chin dart ⌐
⊤ neck ⌐ dart
⌐ edge ⊤

← maximum stretch →

NECK COVER
Cut 2
Windsor Comfort

WIG BACK
Cut 1
Long black fur fabric

Stroke of pile
↓

nape

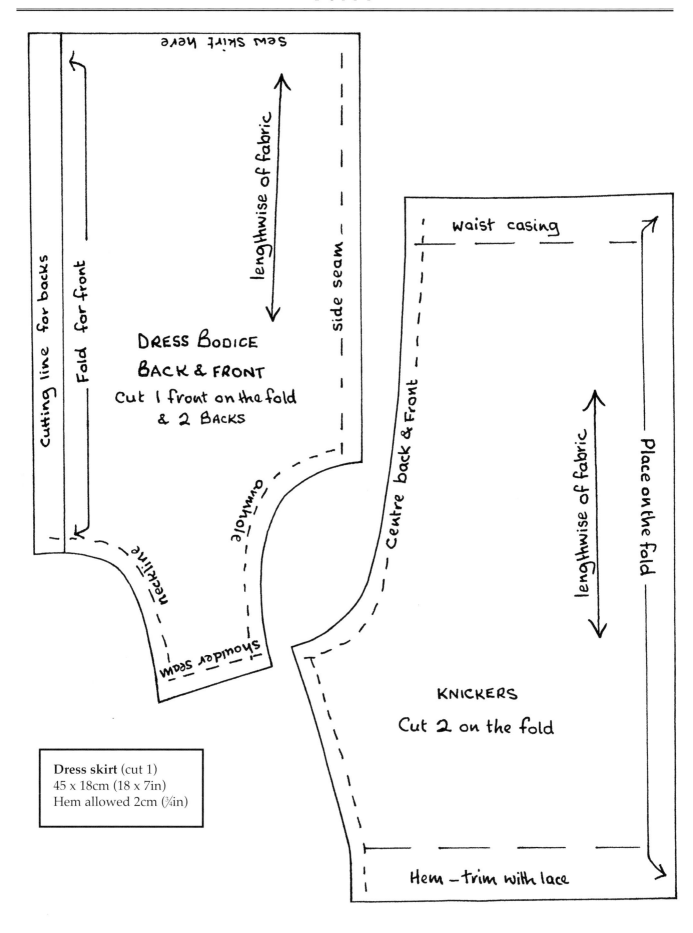

Sew skirt here

lengthwise of fabric

Cutting line for backs

Fold for front

side seam

DRESS BODICE
BACK & FRONT
Cut 1 front on the fold
& 2 Backs

armhole

neckline

Shoulder seam

Centre back & Front

waist casing

lengthwise of fabric

Place on the fold

KNICKERS
Cut 2 on the fold

Hem — trim with lace

Dress skirt (cut 1)
45 x 18cm (18 x 7in)
Hem allowed 2cm (¾in)

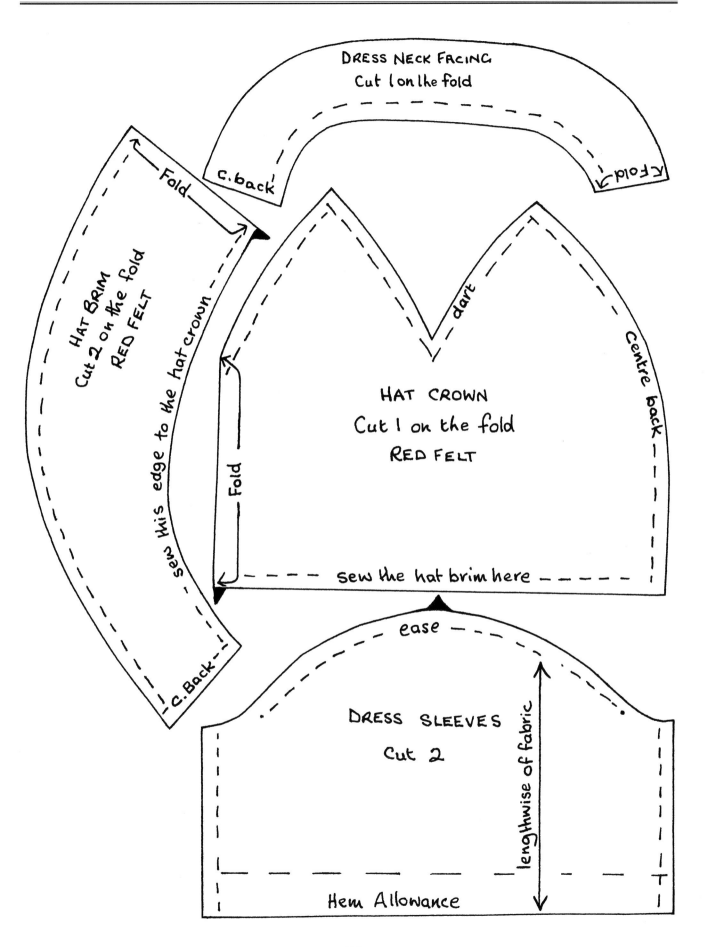

DRESS NECK FACING
Cut 1 on the fold

c.back

Fold

Fold

HAT BRIM
Cut 2 on the fold
RED FELT

sew this edge to the hat crown

dart

Fold

Centre back

HAT CROWN
Cut 1 on the fold
RED FELT

c. Back

sew the hat brim here

ease

DRESS SLEEVES
Cut 2

lengthwise of fabric

Hem Allowance

Melanie and Friends

Melanie and friends are 28cm (11in) dolls, dressed in felt and cotton clothing which is not removable. These small dolls, with their needlesculptured faces and miniature outfits, are popular with both children and collectors.

Materials and equipment

- Flesh- or toast-coloured Windsor Comfort
- Lightweight woven interfacing
- White or cream-coloured thin stockinette (for the socks)
- Long fur fabric, thin knitting wool or mohair roving (for the hair)
- Thin card to make templates of pattern pieces
- White polyester toy filling
- Stuffing sticks
- 2 small buttons and strong thread (for jointing the arms)
- Fabric paints; permanent markers; coloured pencils; cosmetic blusher
- Basic sewing kit, including strong thread and threads to match all fabrics (including those for the clothes)

Clothes

Pants White or cream-coloured thin stockinette; narrow lace trim

Waist petticoats White or cream-coloured cotton or polycotton lawn; lace trim

Dresses Small print or plain cotton

Coats, jackets and hats Felt

Shoes Felt; strong card (for the soles)

Small buttons and beads

Read *Making the Dolls* on pages 8–11 before you begin.

The heads and arms are made from fabric that has a little stretch across the width, and the bodies and legs are made from the same fabric with an iron-on interfacing bonded to the wrong side to prevent stretching. The socks, which are an integral part of the doll, are made from thin stockinette, also interfaced. Windsor Comfort is perfect for small needle sculpture dolls, but any fabric that has a little stretch and does not run may be used. Interfacing must be woven.

The dolls hold small dolls and bears, which you may buy or make yourself.

Making the dolls
To make the head and attach the arms follow the instructions for Poppy (see page 106). The arms are templates, and the fingers are top-stitched.

To make the hairstyles with plaits in wool or mohair see the instructions for Cassie Marie (pages 32–3) and Ginger (page 72).

To needlesculpt and paint the face see the diagrams on page 119 and the face painting guidelines (pages 10–11 and 76–7).

Making the clothes
The clothes were not designed to be removable, but they can be adapted quite easily if you prefer.

To make the felt coats see the needlesculpture baby, Thomas – (pages 86–7). Note that the back-neck facing does not have a centre piece, and the two side facings

join at the centre back. Do not make buttonholes; simply embroider them. Make the collarless jacket as the coat, but omit the collar and buttons.

For the hat see Cassie Marie (page 35).

For all other instructions see the diagrams on the following pages.

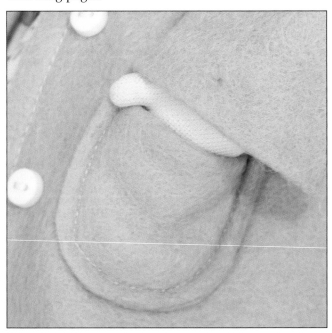

Top-stitch the pockets and collars of the coats in matching or contrasting thread to add interest.

Ruby   **Hollie**   **Penelope**

Ruby wears the full-length coat and beret in red felt with matching T-bar shoes. Her cotton dress has red cherries over a pale green background.

Hollie's jacket is a shortened version of the coat and shows her checked, skirted dress. She wears a beret over her blonde, fur fabric hair and carries a felt shoulder bag to match her ankle-strap shoes.

Penelope has a bright cotton print dress underneath a gold felt collarless jacket and matching hat. The tiny bear tucked in her pocket was once a keyring.

Melanie (page 115) is wearing a full-length coat with matching hat in blue felt and a cotton dress in a dainty, floral print. Her plaited hair is made from blonde mohair roving.

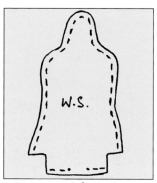

1 Sew around the body, leaving the corners free and an opening between the dots.

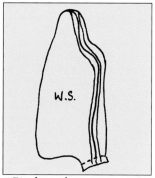

2 Pinch up the corners and, with side seam matching the bottom seam, sew across the corners to make a box shape.

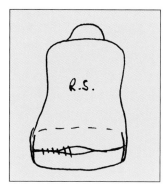

3 Turn R.S. out. Stuff firmly, especially the neck. Ladder-stitch the opening.

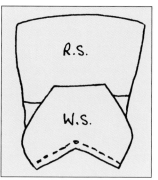

4 With R.S. facing, sew the sock to the leg. With R.S. facing, sew the foot to the sock, matching the dots.

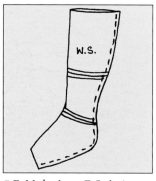

5 Fold the legs, R.S. facing, and sew the centre back seam of leg, sock and foot.

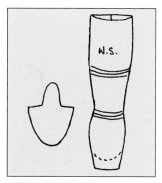

6 Flatten out the feet. Sew around the toes using the guide.

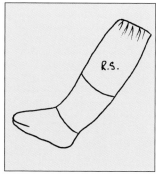

7 Turn the legs R.S. out and stuff firmly to within 1cm (½in) of the tops. Turn in and overcast, gathering slightly to fit the body base.

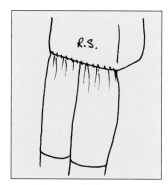

8 Ladder-stitch the legs to the front edge of the body base.

Styling Melanie and Friends' hair

Fur fabric wig
With R.S. facing, sew the centre seam. Turn the wig R.S. out and brush well to release any fur trapped in the seam.

Try the wig on the doll, gathering the edge slightly to fit if necessary, and sew in place.

Style into side pigtails and sew them in place. Sew narrow ribbon bows over the stitches. Trim the fringe.

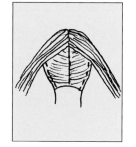

Plaited hairstyle
If using wool, choose a thin-ply yarn. Use black wool with a crinkly texture for Ruby. Follow the instructions for

Cassie Marie's hairstyle (see pages 32–3). Adjust the length of the strands to suit the doll. Make a curly fringe of loops of wool sewn to the forehead for Ruby.

Faces

The faces of all these 28cm (11in) dolls are worked in the same way. When you are needle-modelling a face as small as this, it is impracticable to use specific measurements. Experience will be the best guide, but your first attempts will be a matter of trial and error. On small dolls work with single thread, and instead of using an anchor stitch, secure your thread at the back of the head and take it through to the starting point.

The following nose is most suitable for small dolls. If you use it on larger dolls, work a web of stitches under the stuffing to hold the shape.

1 Needle-model the bridge of the nose and nostrils up to this point as for Thomas (steps 15-18, page 83). Take the thread out at the nostril.

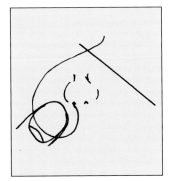

2 Using the point of your needle, pull up a small bump in the stuffing for the nose. Hold the left side in place with your thumb.

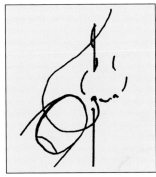

3 Insert the needle at the bridge and take it out at a point just below the nostril, passing the point of the needle over the thread.

4 Pull on the thread to make a loop around the side of the nose.

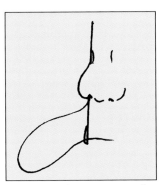

5 Keeping the tension on the thread, stitch up and down to hold it. Do not repeat the loop.

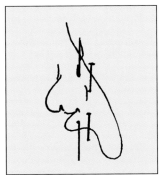

6 When you are modelling the right side of the nose, it is easier to hold the stuffing in place with a straight pin. Loop the thread right around the pin.

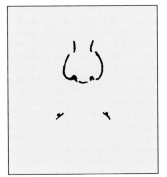

7 Mark the corners of the mouth under the nose and model them (see Thomas, steps 25 and 26, page 84).

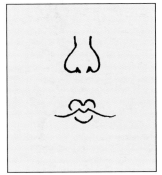

8 Draw the mouth line lightly in tan. Paint the lips or colour them with crayon.

119

9 Draw and paint the eyes. Indent them from the back of the head (see step 7, page 56). Colour the cheeks lightly with cosmetic blusher.

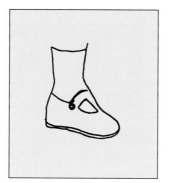

10 T-bar shoe. This is a slip-on shoe, with a bead used as a decorative button fastener. Make the soles in the same way as Amy's shoes (page 19).

11 Ankle-strap shoe. Follow the instructions for Thomas's slippers (page 86). Stitch the straps closed and add a bead for decoration.

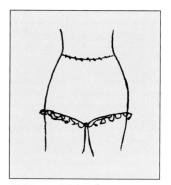

12 Pants. Make the pants without a casing for the elastic. Turn in the raw edge and slipstitch to the doll's waist.

13 Waist petticoat. Sew narrow lace trim to one long edge. Seam the short edges together. Turn in 5mm (¼in) on the waist edge, gather to fit doll and slipstitch in place.

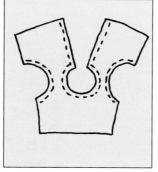

14 Sleeveless dress. With R.S. facing, sew the bodice to the lining along the back edges and around the neckline and along the armholes. Gently turn R.S. out through the shoulders.

15 Sew side seams of bodice and lining. Gather skirt and sew to bodice. Sew the back seam and hem the skirt. Place the dress on the doll and slipstitch the back opening.

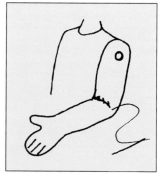

16 If the doll is to hold a small bear or doll, bend the arm at the elbow and ladder-stitch in position before putting on the coat.

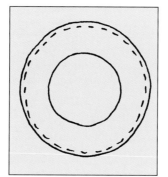

17 Beret. The pattern is a template. Draw around the outer circle on a double layer of felt and machine around on the line. Cut out after sewing. Cut the inner circle from one layer. Turn the beret R.S. out.

18 The beret can be placed at any angle. The hat should be pulled well down. Hats may be sewn in place or left loose.

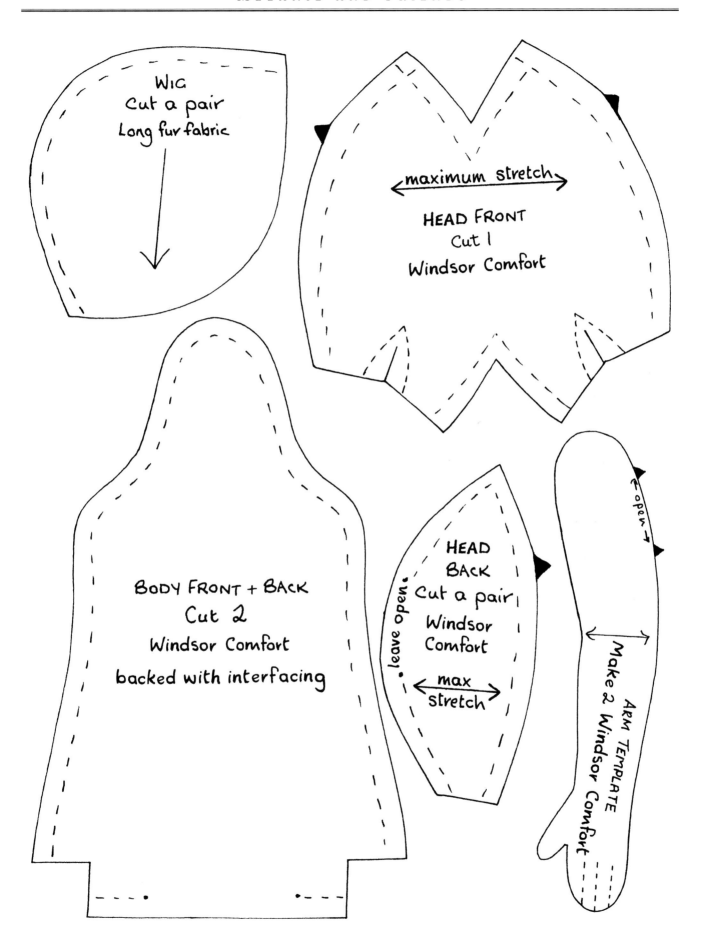

WIG
Cut a pair
Long fur fabric

maximum stretch

HEAD FRONT
Cut 1
Windsor Comfort

BODY FRONT + BACK
Cut 2
Windsor Comfort
backed with interfacing

HEAD
BACK
Cut a pair
Windsor
Comfort

leave open

max
stretch

open

ARM TEMPLATE
Make 2 Windsor Comfort

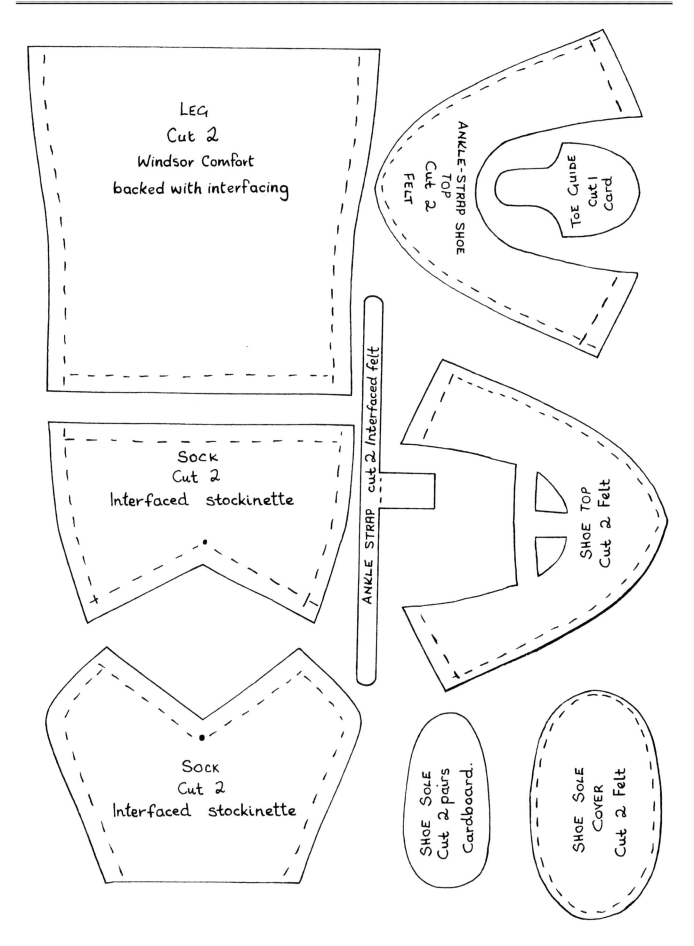

LEG
Cut 2
Windsor Comfort
backed with interfacing

ANKLE-STRAP SHOE
TOP
Cut 2
FELT

TOE GUIDE
Cut 1
Card

SOCK
Cut 2
Interfaced stockinette

ANKLE STRAP cut 2 Interfaced felt

SHOE TOP
Cut 2 Felt

SOCK
Cut 2
Interfaced stockinette

SHOE SOLE
Cut 2 pairs
Cardboard.

SHOE SOLE
COVER
Cut 2 Felt

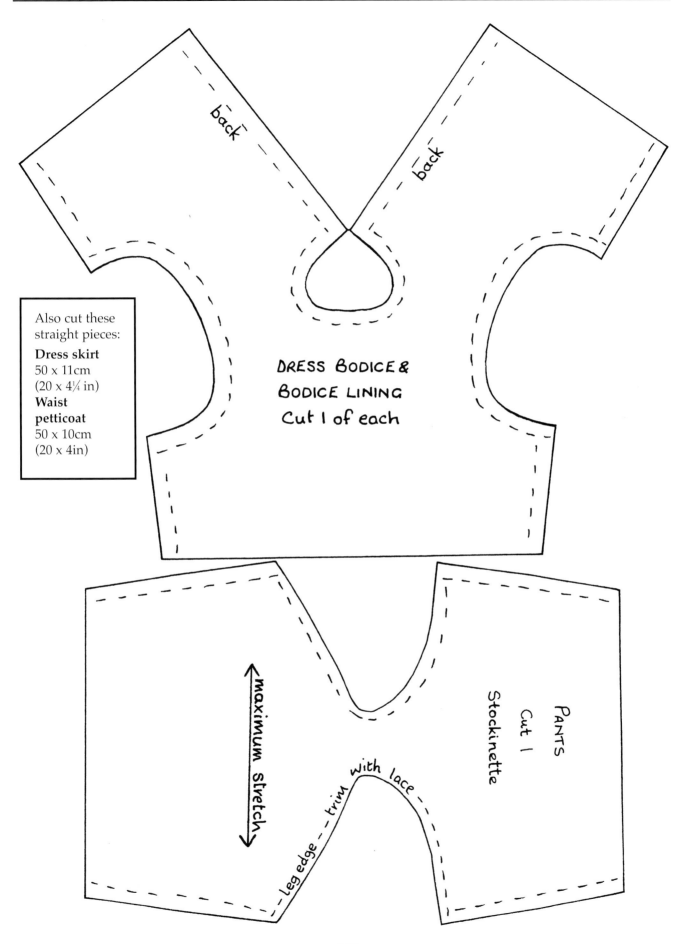

Also cut these
straight pieces:
Dress skirt
50 x 11cm
(20 x 4¼ in)
**Waist
petticoat**
50 x 10cm
(20 x 4in)

back

back

DRESS BODICE &
BODICE LINING
Cut 1 of each

maximum stretch

Leg edge --- trim with lace

PANTS
Cut 1
Stockinette

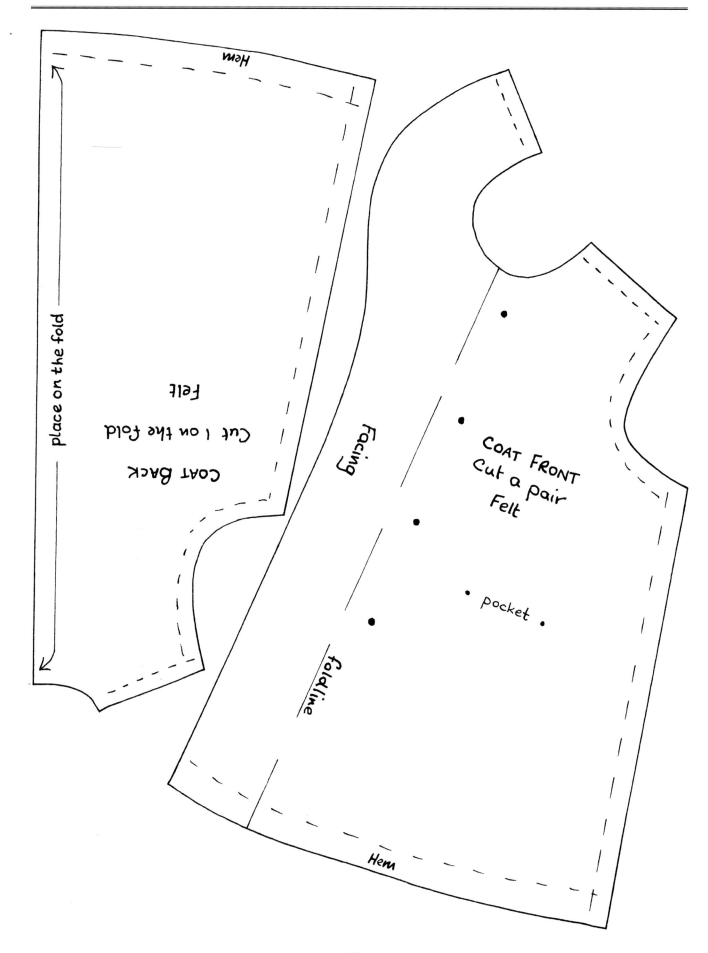

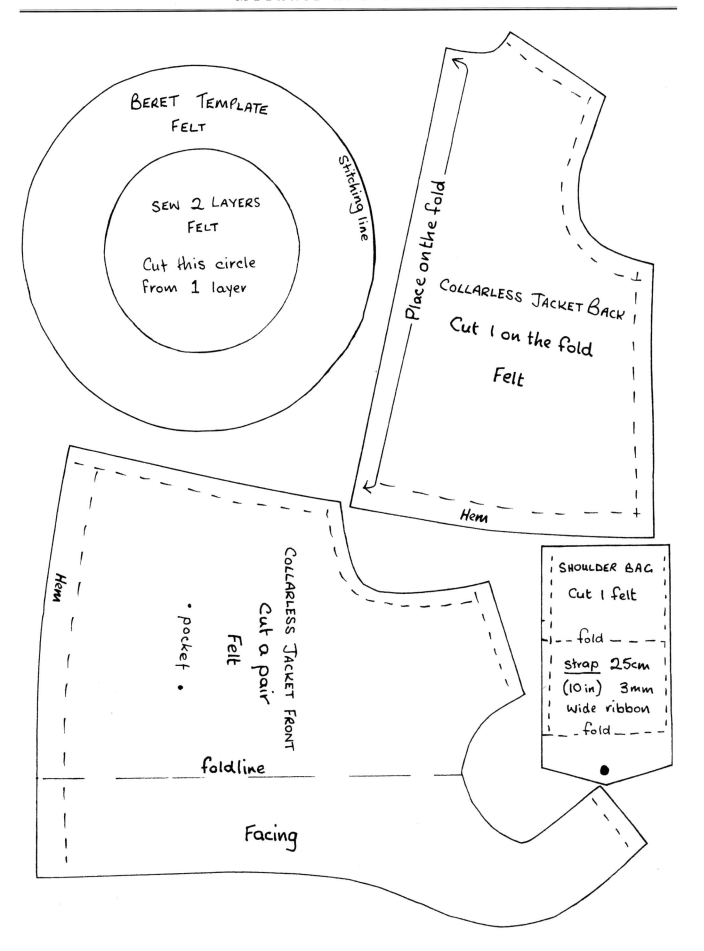

BERET TEMPLATE
FELT

SEW 2 LAYERS
FELT

Cut this circle
from 1 layer

Stitching line

Place on the fold

COLLARLESS JACKET BACK
Cut 1 on the fold
Felt

Hem

Hem

COLLARLESS JACKET FRONT
Cut a pair
Felt

• pocket •

foldline

Facing

SHOULDER BAG
Cut 1 felt

- fold -

strap 25cm
(10 in) 3mm
wide ribbon
fold

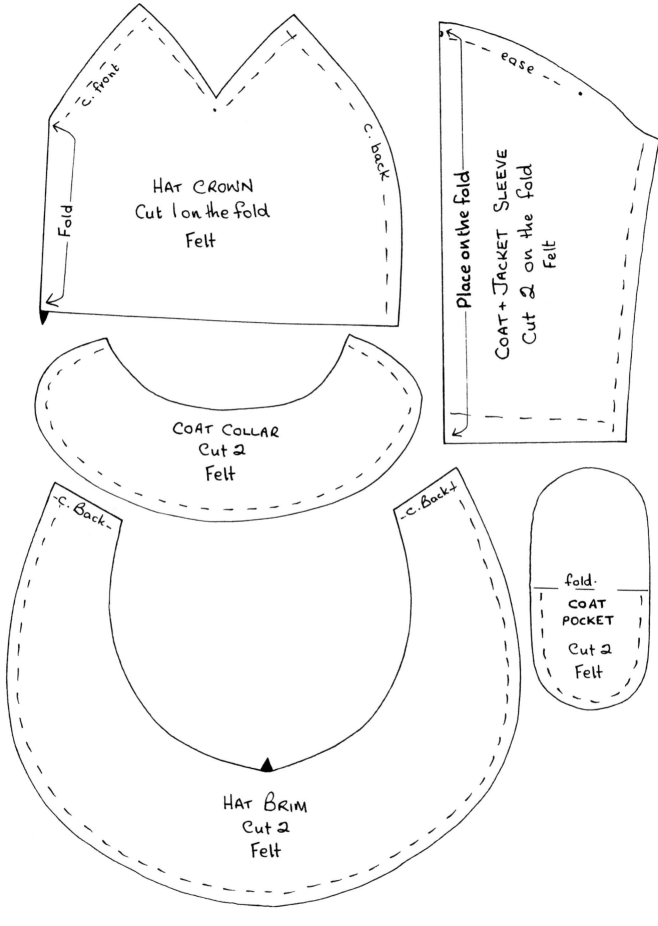

c. front

Fold

HAT CROWN
Cut 1 on the fold
Felt

c. back

ease

Place on the fold

COAT + JACKET SLEEVE
Cut 2 on the fold
Felt

COAT COLLAR
Cut 2
Felt

-c. Back-

c. Back-

HAT BRIM
Cut 2
Felt

fold.

COAT
POCKET

Cut 2
Felt

126

Suppliers

The Internet is an excellent source of mail-order suppliers who are happy to mail their doll-making products worldwide. Following is a selection of the many companies you can find on the Internet. Other US suppliers can be found at www.thedollnet.com.

Calico/stockinette/fur fabric/joints/felt/curly hair/tacky glue

Dainty Supplies Ltd
Unit 35 Phoenix Road
Crowther Industrial Estate
District 3
Washington
Tyne & Wear
NE38 0AD
Tel +44 (0)191 4167886
Website: www.daintysupplies.co.uk
E-mail sales@daintysupplies.com
Shop/mail order/catalogue on request

Stockinette/doll shoes/joints

Recollect Studios
The Old School
London Road
Sayers Common
W Sussex
BN6 9HK
Mail order

Fur fabric/fillings/long needles

Oakley Fabrics
8 May Street
Luton
Bedfordshire
LU1 3QY
Tel +44 (0)1582 734733 / 424828
Mail order/catalogue and samples on request

Calico/Windsor Ponte and Comfort/mohair roving/marker pens/stuffing forks

Sisters & Daughters, Inc.
465 N Burkhart Road
Howell
MI 48843
Tel 1 800 250 5075
Non-US: +1 517 548 5902
Website: www.SistersAndDaughters.com
E-mail: DollSupplies@SistersAnd Daughters.com
Mail order/catalogue on request

Acknowledgements

To my husband, Howard, for his unfailing patience and good humour during the many years he has been chauffeur and handyman to myself and all the dolls.

And to my friends and fellow doll-makers in the Countrywide Dollmakers' Guild, for their encouragement and companionship and for their help in testing my patterns.